HEALTH AND FITNESS IN THE MARTIAL ARTS

HEALTH AND FITNESS IN THE MARTIAL ARTS

BY
Dr. J.C. CANNEY

BATH STREET
p r e s s

Published by:

The Bath Street Press Ltd.
1/5 Bath Street
LONDON
EC1V 9LB

The Bath Street Press
is a subsidiary of Marshall Pickering Holdings Ltd.,
3 Beggarwood Lane, Basingstoke RG23 7LP

British Library Cataloguing in Publication Data
Canney, James C.
   Health and fitness in martial arts.
   1.   Martial arts
   I.   Title
   796.8

ISBN 1-85420-006-2

Edited by David Mitchell
Designed by Jeremy Rose
Illustrated by Martin Lubikowski

Designed and typeset by Positive Productions,
23 Liddell Road Industrial Park,
Maygrove Road, London NW6 2EW.

Printed and bound by Adlard & Son Ltd.,
Letchworth, Herts.

CONTENTS

PAGE

VII

INTRODUCTION

Everyone talks about the fitness needed to practise the martial arts, but where does health come in? What is health anyway?

The man whose sole ambition is to sit in front of the telly all day may well be healthy. The martial artist who wants to be able to train flat out for three minutes without feeling totally exhausted may also be healthy. However, the telly addict is certainly not fit to do what the martial artist can do.

This, I think, is the difference between health and fitness.

A man is healthy if he has a level of fitness which enables him to do what he wants, or needs to do.

The aim of this book is to give the martial arts coach some background knowledge about the body. This will help him to match the physical and mental fitness of students to their wants.

To do this, I have tried to give a (relatively) simple description of how the body is made, and how it works. To this end, I have kept the usage of jargon and technical terminology to a minimum. It has not been possible to do without them completely; not the least reason being that I did not want to have to keep writing "all the muscles on the front of the thighs," when quadriceps would do. All such terms have been written thus, and an explanation is given in the text.

It is unfortunate that any talk about health invariably leads to a discussion about the lack of it! References are made in each section, to some illnesses, injuries etc., which affect the working of the body. I have not however, attempted to give any details of treatment or rehabilitation. What I have done is to describe the principles of this in the hope that the coach will devise exercises and regimes to suit.

In conclusion, I would like to thank David Mitchell for encouraging me to write this book. I also want to thank my wife, Joan, for correcting my often deplorable spelling and grammar.

Chapter 1
NUTRITION

Nutrition is concerned with the fuel required by the body's various motors. That which is taken in as food must be changed into forms which can be absorbed and then used in one of three ways. The first is to provide energy for the necessities of just living. These include:

☐ maintaining a steady body temperature
☐ keeping working such essential muscles as the heart and those involved in breathing.

This is termed 'Basic metabolism'.

The second use is for the renewal and repair of such body tissues as blood and muscle. The third use is to provide the energy needed for other activities such as walking, exercising and working.

The energy used by the body can be measured as heat, using a unit called the 'calorie'. This is the amount of heat needed to raise the temperature of 1 gramme of water by 1 degree centigrade. This is much too small a value to be useful, so we use a unit of 1,000 calories called the 'Kilocalorie', 'kCal', or simply Cal.

Measured in this way, an individual's daily needs amount to about 2,000 Cals for basic metabolism. Actually the basic metabolic rate varies according to a person's surface area, and is lower in women and in older people. Additionally, about 600 Cals are needed for other activities. However, a martial artist in training may need as much as 4,500 Cals per day. All this comes from the food he eats.

Food contains 5 different elements. These are:

☐ carbohydrates
☐ fats
☐ proteins
☐ vitamins & minerals

To these must be added water.

The first 3 categories provide all the energy needed by the body.

CARBOHYDRATES

All food contains the elements carbon, hydrogen and oxygen and carbohydrates are made from these three elements alone. Carbohydrates are built up into large compounds from smaller basic units which are known as 'Sugars' or *Saccharides*.

The simplest carbohydrates are called *Monosaccharides*

because they contain only one basic unit. It is in this form that they are absorbed into the body. Glucose and fructose each contain 6 carbon atoms, 6 oxygen atoms and 12 hydrogen atoms. Galactose contains the same number of atoms of each, though it occurs less commonly than the others mentioned. These three monosaccharides are chemically different because the atoms are arranged in a different pattern in each (*Fig. 1*).

Disaccharide carbohydrates contain two basic units chemically joined in such a way that some water is lost. They therefore consist of 12 carbon atoms, 11 oxygen atoms and 22 hydrogen atoms (*Fig. 2*). The following are common disaccharides:
- sucrose (table sugar) is made up of 1 glucose and 1 fructose unit
- lactose (milk sugar) is made up of 1 glucose and 1 galactose unit
- maltose (malt sugar) is made from 2 glucose units.

There are also tri- and tetrasaccharides which are of little importance other than in producing flatulence.

Much more important are the *Polysaccharides* which can contain perhaps thousands of glucose units, and which make the various

Fig. 1
Monosaccharide sugars

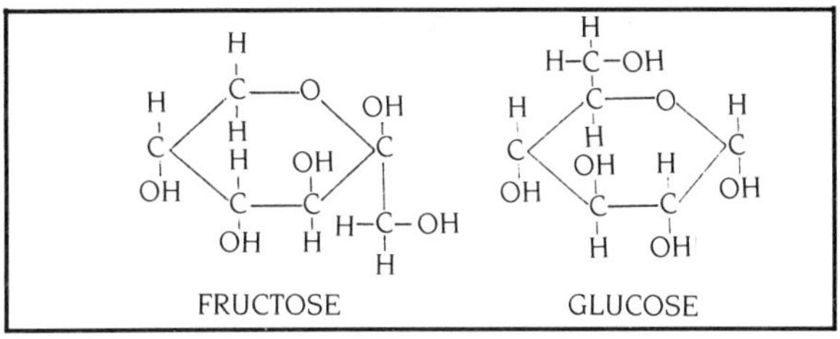

FRUCTOSE   GLUCOSE

Fig. 2
Disaccharide sugars

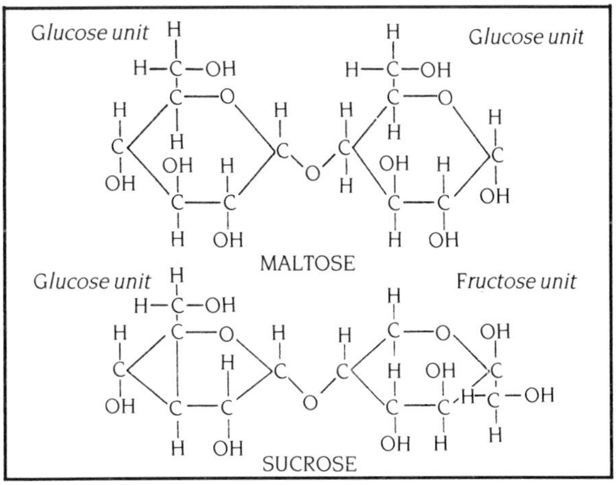

MALTOSE

SUCROSE

'Starches' in the diet. *Glycogen* is unique because it is a poly-saccharide of animal origin - all others come from plants. Glycogen has a relatively simple structure and it is the form in which carbohydrates are stored by the body in the liver and muscle.

FAT

Most of the fat we eat in our diet is made up of Glycerol (usually called 'Glycerin') and fatty acids. These too contain carbon, oxygen and hydrogen, arranged into chains of four or more even numbers of carbon atoms (*Fig. 3*). Glycerol has three carbon atoms, each of which can combine with a fatty acid to form a *Triglyceride* (*Fig. 4*).

Other fats in the diet are what are called *Phospholipids*, where one fatty acid in a triglyceride is replaced by a phosphorous-containing compound. *Sterols* are fatty acids attached to a more complex base, , the best known being *Cholesterol*. Other sterols are vitamins A and D, and the steroid hormones.

A great deal of fuss is nowadays made over 'Saturated' and 'Unsaturated' fats. This term simply refers to whether a fatty acid has its maximum number of hydrogen atoms - in which case it is said to be 'Saturated', or has less than maximum - in which case it is

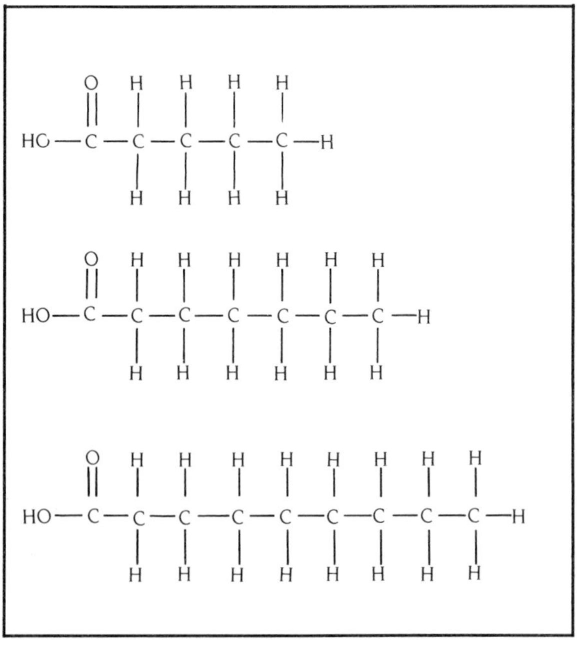

Fig. 3
Fatty acids

said to be 'Unsaturated' (*Fig. 5*). The respective values or dangers of these two types of fat are probably exaggerated, and a mixture of both in moderate amounts in the diet is best.

Three unsaturated fatty acids are referred to as 'Essential'. This is based upon the fact that certain animals do not grow as well as they should when fed on a diet which excludes them. However there is no evidence that this applies to human beings.

PROTEINS

Proteins are made up of carbon, oxygen and hydrogen plus nitrogen. In many cases proteins also contain minerals such as iron, phosphorus or sulphur. Proteins are very large molecules which are built up from simple units named *Aminoacids*. When two aminoacids link together, the result is a *Peptide* (*Fig. 6*); two or more peptides link together to form a *Polypeptide*, and each protein is in turn comprised of many polypeptides. A protein may contain many thousand aminoacid units!

Aminoacids can link together in a number of ways so the resulting proteins can have almost unlimited structures. These include parallel interlocking chains, corkscrew-shaped chains ('Helices'),

Fig. 4
A Triglyceride

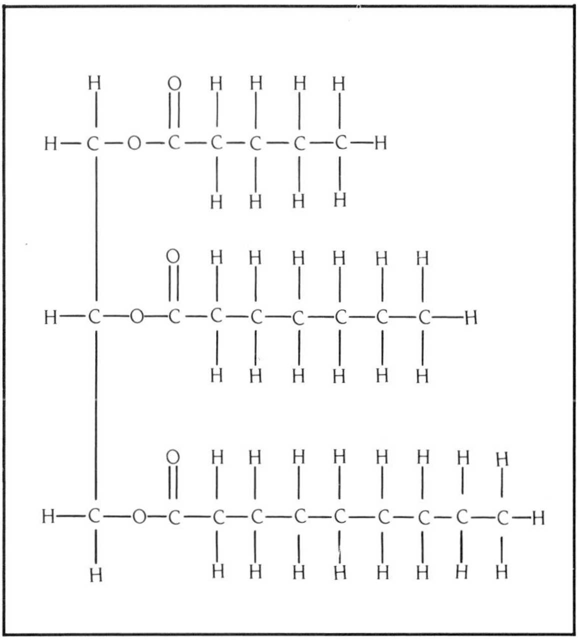

or random combinations of shapes (*Fig. 7*).

Each body tissue has its own specific protein. DNA ('Deoxy-ribonucleic acid') protein is the blueprint for every living creature - human or otherwise. It determines whether Bill has buck teeth, Jill has red hair, or Bob really is a boy. Each molecule of DNA is shaped like a double inter-connected helix made up from many thousands of aminoacid units and maybe as many as 500,000,000 nitrogen atoms.

Only twenty-three aminoacids are of importance, and ten of these are essential for health. Protein is divided into first and second class. Animal protein is first class and contains all the essential aminoacids. Vegetable protein is second class and does not contain all the essential aminoacids. It therefore follows that it is very difficult, if not impossible to design a satisfactory 100% vegetable ('Vegan') diet. Some animal-derived protein - such as

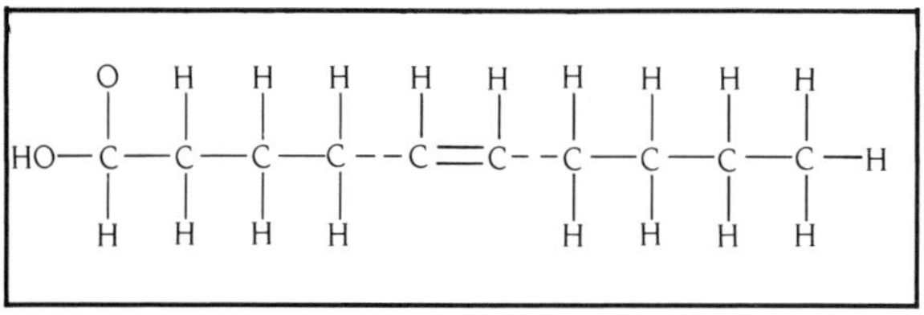

Fig. 5
Unsaturated fatty acid

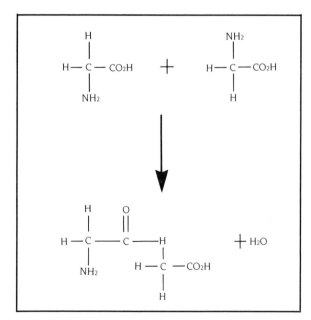

Fig. 6
Two simple amino acids link to form a peptide

that from dairy produce, meat, fish, or eggs - is necessary for a nutritionally satisfactory diet.

VITAMINS

Neither vitamins nor minerals actually provide energy yet both are nevertheless essential for health. Vitamins are necessary to the workings of the body and their lack from the diet causes various diseases. This discovery was first made in the 18th century when it was found that scurvy amongst seamen was prevented by including fruit or fruit juices into their diet. It is now known that this introduced Vitamin C into a diet which was almost wholly lacking it.

Vitamins are divided into two types - fat soluble and water soluble. Fat soluble vitamins are A, D, E and K. These need a certain amount of fat to carry them into the blood from the intestine. They dissolve in the body fat and considerable supplies are stored in

Fig. 7
Proteins can have the following structures: Helix; Parallel chain or Random chain

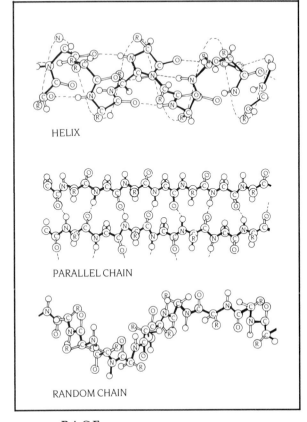

HELIX

PARALLEL CHAIN

RANDOM CHAIN

this way. This means that deficiency symptoms take a long time to appear, but it also means that vitamin poisoning can occur.

Vitamin A is found in animal and fish livers, and in most meat and vegetables. There is little in dairy produce. This vitamin achieved fame in the last war because it was thought to improve night vision. It does however, do other things as well. Lack of Vitamin A causes a roughness and soreness of the skin. It may also cause dryness of the eyes, leading to severe eye infections from which blindness can result. Vitamin A poisoning shows as loss of appetite, dry and itchy skin, and painful swellings in the arms and legs. Acute poisoning can produce symptoms of drowsiness, headache, vomiting, itching and peeling of the skin.

Vitamin D is found in oily fish such as herring and sardines. It also occurs in most dairy produce though there is little in meat and vegetables. Vitamin D is produced in the body by the action of sunlight on sterols which occur naturally in the skin. Therefore it is not an essential part of the diet in many parts of the world. However, people who spend most of their time indoors will need Vitamin D in their diet.

Vitamin D is necessary for the absorbtion of the calcium which gives bone its hardness. Lack of Vitamin D causes the bones to soften, producing a condition in children known as 'Rickets'. Vitamin D overdosage is more often seen in babies but it can also occur in adults. Symptoms are loss of appetite, vomiting, severe thirst, bowel disorders, loss of weight and irritability. If the overdosage continues, the result is eventual coma and death.

Vitamin E is necessary in the diets of certain animals such as dogs, rabbits, some monkeys and particularly chickens. No clear function for Vitamin E has been found in humans but it is known to prevent the oxidation of fats - a process which makes them rancid - and it may possibly have a similar function in the body.

Lack of Vitamin K in the diet does not seem to cause any ill-effects though it does play a part in the process of blood clotting.

Vitamins B and C are water soluble. Neither is stored in the body and that which is not used immediately, is excreted unchanged in the urine.

Vitamin C is found in fresh fruit and most fresh vegetables but there is little in meat and dairy produce. Vitamin C has already been referred to in connection with scurvy. This disease starts with listlessness and weakness, followed by swelling and bleeding from the gums. Bleeding under the skin also occurs and if allowed to continue, death results.

Vitamin C is necessary for the making of those substances which glue the cells and tissues of the body together.

The best source of vitamins in the B group is brewers' yeast. Other good sources are bran, wholewheat flour, bread, nuts and pork. Other foods contain very little of this vitamin. Vitamin B was eventually found to be a mixture of different substances, each of which is concerned in some way with the chemical reactions by which the body functions. Lack of this vitamin complex causes a great variety of diseases, including neuritis (inflammation or degeneration of the nerves), dermatitis (inflammation of the skin) digestive disorders and various types of anaemia.

Fat soluble vitamins are very stable. Water soluble vitamins are easily destroyed - particularly by heat or long periods of storage. They are not stored in the body and any surplus is got rid of, primarily in the urine.

The daily vitamin requirement is very small and even a balanced weight reduction diet of just 800 Cals per day contains enough.

It follows that vitamin supplements are not necessary for martial artists who are already taking a good balanced diet. Such supplements may result in Vitamins A and D poisoning whilst otherwise producing expensive urine!

MINERALS

Life originated in the sea, though most martial art practice nowadays takes place on dry land! Consequently the whole of body chemistry is based on a saline (salty) environment. A major preoccupation of the body lies in accurately maintaining its salt/water balance.

Necessary minerals such as sodium and potassium chlorides are so widely found that even the best 'salt-free diets' contain an adequate daily supply of them! But, martial artists training in hot and/or humid conditions lose a lot of salt in sweat and if this is not replaced, heat exhaustion, lethargy, headache and vomiting can result. Replacement can be made by taking salt tablets, or by adding salt to food or drinks. Under these circumstances, salt in your beer or coke tastes very good!

Many other minerals are essential in trace amounts. Iron for example, is a constituent of haemoglobin, the oxygen-carrying part of blood. Iodine is an essential part of thyroid hormone which controls metabolic rate. The mineral calcium makes bone hard. Still other minerals are needed in minute quantities but the starvation diet referred to before contains adequate amounts of all these.

WATER

Water is not a food but it is necessary to maintain the body's saline environment. Besides this, it has three other functions:
- it dissolves excess minerals which might be in the diet and which would be poisonous if they remained in the body
- it dissolves the waste products of aminoacid breakdown, excreting these with surplus minerals, in the form of urine
- it evaporates as sweat from the skin, and thereby maintains a constant internal body temperature.

More than 50% of solid food is water but most or all of this is balanced by the volume of digestive juices needed to break the food down; so the nett gain is nil. Other sources of water are drinks such as tea, coffee, squashes, plain water itself, or beer - but not milk!

The amount of water lost in the urine is normally about two litres per day, though it is never less than one litre. The volume of water lost as sweat varies with the air temperature, humidity, and the amount of physical work being done. An office worker in a cool environment will lose about one and a half litres whilst a martial artist training hard in the tropics may lose as much as fifteen litres.

When balanced out, the average person needs to drink between two, and two-and-a-half litres of water to day. The martial artist mentioned above will need this volume, plus the amount lost in sweat. This means an intake of between fifteen to twenty litres per day! This should be taken in the form of small amounts - perhaps only sips all day - as he/she is training.

THE PROCESS OF DIGESTION

To make energy available from food, it must first be digested by the body (*Fig. 8*).

It is easy to get at the energy available from a piece of bread, for example. All you need to do is set it on fire, and its energy is given up as heat. The body has to do the same thing but without using fire - and this is more complicated. The mixture of substances which we call a piece of bread has to undergo many stages in the body before it finishes up as carbon dioxide and water. Each of these stages is carried out using *Enzymes*. Enzymes are substances already in the body and which are unchanged by the reaction they are involved with.

The process of digestion starts when food is put in the mouth and chewed. This breaks it into small pieces and mixes it with digestive enzymes. A little absorbtion of carbohydrates occurs in the mouth. When swallowed, the chewed up food passes down to the stomach where it is mixed with more enzymes and with acid produced by glands which line the stomach.

Fig. 8
Digestive system

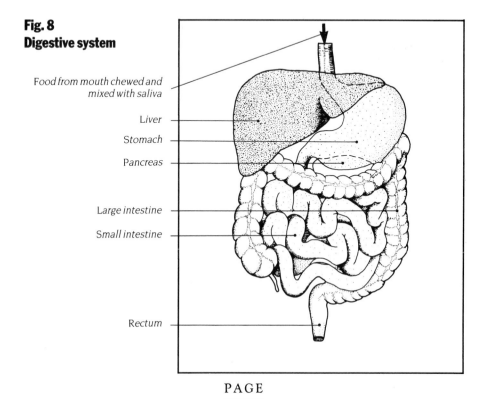

Food from mouth chewed and mixed with saliva

Liver

Stomach

Pancreas

Large intestine

Small intestine

Rectum

From the stomach, the food passes into the small bowel where first the acid is neutralised by bile from the liver, then it is mixed with yet more enzymes, this time from the pancreas. This mixture moves on through all 20 feet of the small bowel as the process of digestion continues.

All starches are broken down during digestion into maltose, and then into glucose. Glucose is the form in which carbohydrates are absorbed into the bloodstream. It is stored in the liver as glycogen, and in other tissues as compounds of glucose or fat.

The liver converts some glucose into glycogen and stores it there. The remaining glucose is changed and stored in other body tissues. For example, fat cells store converted glucose as fat.

Digestion breaks fats down into glycerol and free fatty acids. Glycerol is soluble in water and so is absorbed. The free fatty acids form soaps with bile to aid their absorbtion.

Free fatty acids are used by all tissues, including the brain, as an immediate source of energy. They give twice as much energy as an equivalent weight of glucose but only survive in the blood for a few minutes before being filtered out and rebuilt into triglycerides for storage in the body's 'Adipose' (fatty) tissue. They are released from there in the form of fatty acids when the need arises.

The process of digestion splits all proteins - no matter how complicated or large - into individual aminoacid units. Protein digestion and absorbtion occurs in the stomach and small intestine.

Aminoacids have a more varied fate. All body protein is in a constant cycle of breakdown and renewal. As much as 100 grammes of body protein are broken down each day and the aminoacids liberated by this process join those from digested food to form a common pool from which replacement protein is made up.

A certain amount of protein is lost during the production of hair, urine and faeces. Deficiencies are made up by dietary aminoacids. During periods of growth or recovery from injury, more protein is built up than is broken down. Surplus protein is broken down by means of a process which actually yields energy. Nitrogen from protein breakdown is released in the form of urea.

DIET & TRAINING

In the introduction to this chapter, it was said that the body's energy requirements vary from between 2,500 Cals for a sedentary worker, to about 4,500 Cals for a martial artist who is training hard.

Each food has a different energy value. Protein and carbohydrate each yield about 4 Cals per gramme whilst fat gives more than twice that at 9 Cals per gramme.

The diet needed to furnish energy for training must be 'Balanced', that is to say it must contain the correct proportions of the various food constituents for healthy working of the body. Martial artists need to take around 30% of their diet as protein, and this should contain adequate amounts of the essential aminoacids.

High protein diets have no special benefits because surplus protein is used to provide energy which can be better supplied from carbohydrates or fats. The martial artist who trains exclusively on a diet of steak will have little more than constipation to show for his efforts.

The rest of the body's energy needs are met by carbohydrate and fat, though the relative proportions of each in the diet are a matter of debate which is at times, acrimonious. A certain amount of fat is necessary to provide the essential fatty acids and to act as a carrier for the fat soluble vitamins. It is likely that the fat contained in the average diet yields 10% of the energy needed but if more energy is required, more fat should be taken in. In my opinion, martial artists could obtain up to 30% of their energy requirements from fat.

The remaining 40 - 60% must be provided by carbohydrates. Practically all foods contain some carbohydrate but vegetables and cereals provide most. These also provide the majority of fibre, or 'roughage' in the diet. Fibre is mainly made up from *Cellulose*, a group of carbohydrates containing 3,000 or more glucose units arranged in such ways that the digestive enzymes cannot break down. Some digestion does occur through the action of bacteria which grow in the intestine. Fibre actually feeds these germs, which is just as well since they are necessary for health.

High fibre diets are fashionable, and certainly the average diet contains too little. However as usual, excess is bad and too much fibre stops the absorbtion of calcium, iron and other minerals.

Ordinary sugar has little to recommend it other than being pleasant to eat. Having said that, it can provide a rapid boost to blood glucose levels so it is useful to a martial artist requiring a very rapid source of of energy - such as during a competition or grading. However under ordinary circumstances, too much sugar can put a strain on the body's regulating mechanisms.

A teaspoonful of sugar will provide a high level of potential energy over a period of perhaps 30 - 45 minutes. An apple provides the same amount of energy but over a 2 to 3 hour period.

To summarise therefore, a martial artist in training will need a diet yielding 4,500 Cals. of energy, of which 30% is protein derived, 10 - 30% from fat, and 40 - 60% from carbohydrate which contains a reasonable amount of fibre. This diet should contain adequate amounts of vitamins and minerals, without the need for supplementary pills and potions.

Chapter 2
RESPIRATION

RESPIRATION

Having got the fuel into the body by means of the digestive system, it is then necessary to provide oxygen so that its energy can be released. Respiration is the process by which oxygen is carried from the air, to the organs that use it. Not only that, but 'burning' of the fuel releases the waste products carbon dioxide and water, and these must be removed.

Basically, the process of respiration can be expressed as follows:
- air is taken into the lungs, and oxygen passes into the blood
- the oxygen is transported to the organs (or 'Tissues'), where it is used to 'burn' the fuel
- the carbon dioxide waste product passes into the blood
- the carbon dioxide is returned to the lungs and breathed out into the air (*Fig. 9*).

Two body systems are involved in respiration. These are:
1. the lungs
2. the body fluids

THE LUNGS
The lungs are two large organs situated in the chest, at the lower end of what is called 'the Respiratory Tract' (breathing apparatus).

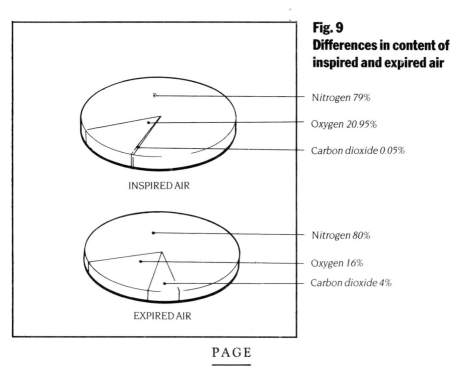

Fig. 9
Differences in content of inspired and expired air

Nitrogen 79%

Oxygen 20.95%

Carbon dioxide 0.05%

INSPIRED AIR

Nitrogen 80%

Oxygen 16%

Carbon dioxide 4%

EXPIRED AIR

Air first enters through the nose, passing through the back of the mouth and voice box (*Larynx*). and entering the windpipe (*Trachea*). This is a wide tube which is held permanently open by rings of cartilage.

The trachea divides into two *Bronchi* (singular - *Bronchus*), one going to each lung. The walls of the bronchi contain elastic tissue and muscle fibres. The fibres close the tubes when they contract and the pull of the elastic tissue makes the lungs smaller (*Fig. 10*).

The bronchi divide into smaller and smaller tubes, the smallest called *Bronchioles*, until they lead finally into blind ending air sacs (*Alveoli*). Here the air is brought into intimate contact with the blood.

The air is warmed to body temperature and moistened as it passes through the nose, larynx, trachea and bronchi.

The mechanics of breathing depends upon two things. Firstly it depends upon contraction of the muscles of the chest wall and diaphragm when breathing in ('Inspiration'), and secondly upon the elasticity of the lungs during breathing out ('Expiration').

The chest (*Thorax*) in which the lungs are situated is air-tight. It is bounded on the sides and top by chest wall. This consists of the

Fig. 10
The respiratory system

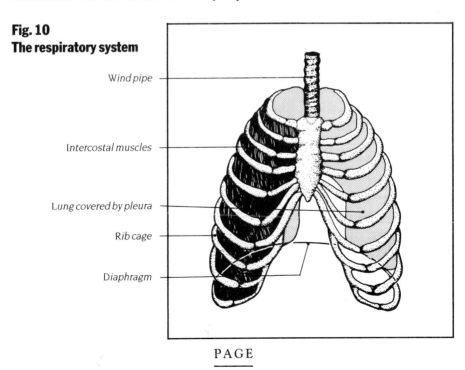

Wind pipe

Intercostal muscles

Lung covered by pleura

Rib cage

Diaphragm

ribs which are joined together by muscles known as *Intercostals*, and below by the large band of muscle which is the diaphragm. The latter muscle separates the thorax from the abdomen. The chest is lined by a lubricating membrane called the *Pleura*. This allows the lungs to slide easily on the chest wall (*see Fig. 10*).

The diaphragm contracts on inspiration, pushing down the abdominal organs. At the same time, the intercostal muscles contract, lifting and rotating the ribs. The effect of both these actions is to increase the volume inside the chest, expanding the lungs and creating a partial vacuum into which air is sucked via the breathing passages.

The diaphragm relaxes during expiration, allowing the abdominal contents to push it up. At the same time the intercostal muscles relax, and the elasticity of the lungs pulls them smaller, so air is driven out.

The normal breathing rate whilst resting is about 15 per minute, i.e., each breath cycle takes about 4 seconds. During this time, about half a litre of air is inhaled and then exhaled. By breathing in fully at the top of a resting breath, an extra two and a half litres of air can be inhaled. At the end of expiration, another one and a half litres can be exhaled by contracting the abdominal muscles so the diaphragm is pushed upwards. These therefore give a reserve of four litres, so the normal maximum volume of air which can be taken in per cycle is about four and a half litres.

An important factor is the volume of the respiratory tract where oxygen is not in close contact with the blood. This occurs in the nose, mouth, trachea, bronchi and bronchioles and is known as the 'dead space'.

Actually only about 70% of the air breathed at rest is useable. The 150 mls in the dead space remains constant, no matter how deeply you breathe.

At rest, the volume of useable air passing through the lungs will be around 0.3 multiplied by 15, or 5.25 litres per minute. If you now take a little exercise and your breathing rate doubles, the volume of useable air becomes 0.3 multiplied by 30, or 10.5 litres per minute.

You could of course double the volume of each breath, in which case the useable air would be 1 minus 0.15, or 0.85 litres which, at the original breathing rate is 0.85 multiplied by 15, giving 12.75 litres per minute. In other words, deeper and slower breathing is more efficient than fast, shallow breathing.

At rest, the body uses approximately 8 litres of air per minute but during exercise, this may rise to 150 litres, or even 200 litres if training is really intense. The nose cannot cope with rates above 50 litres per minute, so the martial artist has to resort to mouth breathing. This can lead to problems in that the inspired air is neither warmed nor moistened to the same degree and this leads to dryness of the air passages. Occasionally this results in pain being felt behind the breastbone. This is of no significance but it does indicate some irritation of the trachea as the latter becomes too dry.

THE BODY FLUIDS

There are 3 different types of body fluid:
- blood plasma; this is the fluid part of the blood
- interstitial ('Between tissues') fluid bathes all the body cells
- intracellular fluid is inside the cells themselves.

Over half the body weight is made up of fluid and in a 70 kilo individual, about 35 kilos are intracellular fluid, 16 kilos are interstitial fluid and 4 kilos are blood plasma (*Fig. 11*).

Blood is the transport system by which oxygen and nutrients are distributed to the tissues, and waste products are removed. Blood consists of cells and plasma, the latter making up 55-60% of blood volume.

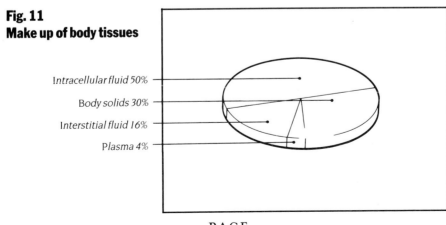

Fig. 11
Make up of body tissues

Intracellular fluid 50%
Body solids 30%
Interstitial fluid 16%
Plasma 4%

There are 3 kinds of blood cell:
□ red blood cells, or corpuscles ('RBCs')
□ white blood cells ('WBCs')
□ platelets.

RBCs are responsible for transporting oxygen. They do this by means of the substance called *Haemoglobin*. This is a very large molecule made up of 4 identical sub-units. Each sub-unit is a compound of *Haem*, and a polypeptide (remember those?). Haem contains one iron atom and this is capable of carrying one molecule of oxygen. Therefore each molecule of haemoglobin can transport four molecules of oxygen and when it does, it is called *Oxyhaemoglobin*.

The way in which oxygen associates with haemoglobin is peculiar in that it neither reacts with the haemoglobin, nor is it dissolved in it. The result however is that oxygen is taken up very

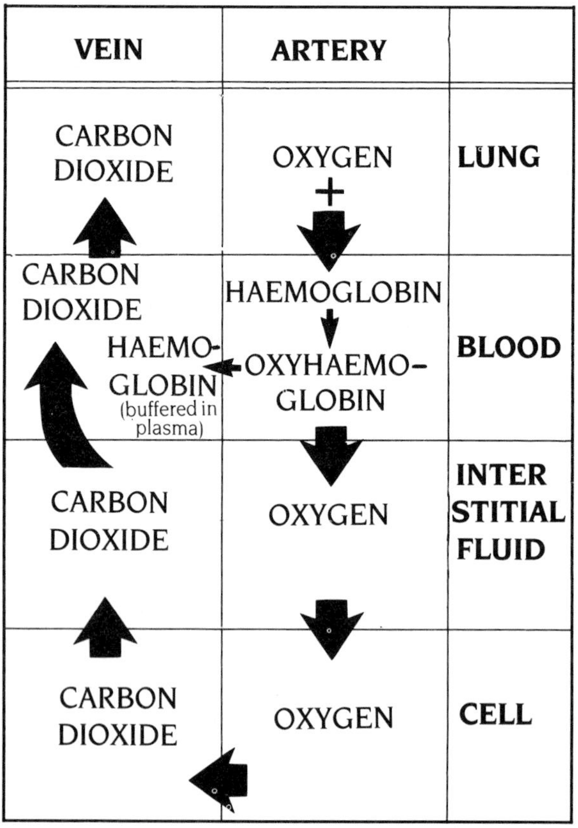

VEIN	ARTERY	
CARBON DIOXIDE ↑	OXYGEN + ↓	LUNG
CARBON DIOXIDE HAEMO-GLOBIN (buffered in plasma) ↰	HAEMOGLOBIN ↓ OXYHAEMO-GLOBIN ↓	BLOOD
CARBON DIOXIDE ↑	OXYGEN ↓	INTER STITIAL FLUID
CARBON DIOXIDE ↰	OXYGEN	CELL

Fig. 12
Oxygen is absorbed by the body in the form of Oxyhaemoglobin and carbon dioxide expelled

rapidly by the blood, in about one hundredth of a second. When the oxyhaemoglobin reaches the tissues, the oxygen it contains passes first into the interstitial fluid and from thence into the cells themselves (*Fig. 12*).

Haemoglobin is blue in colour but when it takes up oxygen, it becomes bright red. That is why the blood in veins is darker than that in arteries - it contains less oxygen.

When fully saturated, each gramme of oxyhaemoglobin is carrying 1.34 mls of oxygen. The average concentration of haemoglobin is 15 grammes per 100 mls of blood, so each 100 mls of blood can carry about 20 mls of oxygen.

In practice, oxygenated blood going to the tissues is only about 97% saturated whilst that returning from resting tissues is about 75% saturated. The tissues are therefore taking about 4.6 mls of oxygen from each 100 mls of blood. This adds up to a total resting tissue uptake of around a quarter litre per minute.

Since the blood can never carry more oxygen than it does at rest, it is of no value to breathe pure oxygen, or to over-breathe before training. In fact this can be positively harmful because it washes too much carbon dioxide from the blood.

Oxygen is given up by oxyhaemoglobin for 3 main reasons:
□ firstly there is less oxygen in the tissues so a simple
  physical equalisation takes place
□ secondly the tissues contain a higher concentration of carbon
  dioxide. This is acidic, and haemoglobin cannot carry as much
  oxygen in an acid environment
□ thirdly an increase in temperature makes the oxyhaemoglobin
  split into oxygen and haemoglobin.

A proper warm up which slightly raises the temperature of working tissues therefore speeds up the rate at which oxygen passes into them.

As I have said, oxygen is used in the tissues to burn the fuel and provide energy. Waste water from this process passes into the interstitial fluid where it is used in the maintaining of the body's fluid balance. Most carbon dioxide passes through the RBCs where enzymes change it into a form which dissolves easily in the blood plasma. This however, would make the blood acidic - something which the body simply cannot tolerate - were it not for a reservoir of substances capable of neutralising it.

The neutralising substances are made up of proteins in both the plasma and the RBCs. They are known as 'Buffers' and will be discussed when we come to consider the internal respiration of muscle cells.

Dissolved carbon dioxide is carried back to the lungs, where it passes into the air sacs and is breathed out (*see Fig. 12*).

There are about 5 - 10,000 WBCs per ml of blood. WBCs are of several different types but all are concerned with defence and repair. The body must be protected from certain bacteria and viruses which cause illness, then the damage which they have done must be repaired.

First reaction to infection or injury is 'Inflammation'. This is an increase in local blood flow and is most easily seen in a skin infection such as a boil, where the extra blood makes the skin red. This helps to wall off the infection as far as possible, whilst at the same time increasing the number of WBCs. These move into the affected area and consume living germs and dead tissue. In the case of a boil, the end result of this process is *Pus*.

Once the damaged area has been cleaned up, the process of repair begins. Remaining tissues are glued together by clotting of the interstitial fluid in a process which takes three to four days. This in turn is followed by a growth of fibrous tissue into the clot to produce a solid joining. The whole process can take twelve or more weeks.

Some WBCs can confer immunity against foreign substances by producing proteins called 'Antibodies'. These recognise and neutralise foreign proteins known as *Antigens*. The WBCs must learn how to do this for each particular antigen, and this is how the body develops immunity to such diseases as measles (it is rare to have more than one attack). It also explains why immunisation works against diseases such as *Tetanus* ('Lockjaw').

Antibodies circulate in the blood but can also attach themselves to various tissue cells. When the circulating antibody level is low, antigens attach to tissue cells and damage them. This results in an allergic condition of varying intensity - from relatively mild hayfever, to complete collapse of the circulation and death.

Platelets are small cells concerned with clotting. When a blood vessel is damaged, platelets stick to the injured area and produce a substance called *Fibrin*. This binds the platelets together and traps other blood vessels, so forming a clot which quickly hardens and seals the hole. However, if damage occurs to the lining of an artery (*Arterio-sclerosis*), then the artery can become blocked by a blood clot (*Thrombosis*) and when this occurs in the heart, a *Coronary thrombosis* or heart attack results.

EFFECTS OF EXERCISE

An increase in muscle activity brings about an increase in the volume of carbon dioxide generated and passed into the blood. This plus the higher temperature of the working muscles increases the rate at which oxygen is given up by the blood. Therefore the mere fact of muscle activity automatically produces the changes necessary to maintain that activity.

More muscle activity leads to more carbon dioxide produced, and this in turn leads to more oxygen released to the muscles.

This is well seen by the fact that oxygen levels in blood coming from the muscles can fall from the 75% resting level to only 15 - 20% during exercise. This means that more haemoglobin is available in the lungs to extract oxygen from the air. An increased level of carbon dioxide causes a faster rate of breathing and this in turn produces a much higher rate of gas exchange between blood and air in the air sacs.

Strangely, training has little effect upon lung function, though chest capacity is sometimes slightly increased. The major improvement is brought about by proper breathing techniques. Efficient operation of the diaphragm and chest muscles during inspiration, and of the abdominal muscles during expiration will improve usage of the lung's reserve capacity.

Cigarette smoking affects training in that haemoglobin has an affinity for carbon monoxide 300 times greater than for oxygen. A smoker will carry carbon monoxide in his blood as *Carboxyhaemoglobin* and this can reach as high as 10%. The effect of this is to leave that much less haemoglobin to carry oxygen. Therefore martial artists who smoke should refrain from doing so for about six hours prior to hard training. By doing this, most of the carboxyhaemoglobin in their blood will have been eliminated.

Total volume of blood in the body is about 5 litres, of which 750 grammes is haemoglobin. These amounts are slightly lower in women. During hard training, the haemoglobin is constantly used to capacity and this leads to an adaptive increase of up to 50% of the total blood volume. This increase is not quite matched by a commensurate increase in RBCs, so the blood appears weaker. It sometimes becomes so weak that the martial artist seems to have anaemia. There is nevertheless a considerable actual increase in the amount of haemoglobin circulating.

There are two ways of artificially increasing the amount of haemoglobin. The first is legal, the second is illegal. Training at high altitude, where there is less oxygen, can increase the level of haemoglobin in the blood by about 20%. This process takes three weeks or so but it does not yield a total gain because the blood becomes thicker and more sticky, so the heart must work harder to pump it around.

Altitude training is essential if competing at significant heights above sea level but it has a doubtful value when competing at normal levels. At least ten days are required for the body to re-acclimatise to the lower level.

The second and illegal way of increasing haemoglobin is 'Blood doping'. This is said to be common in some sports and unfortunately, there is no reliable way of detecting it. The process involves taking some blood from the martial artist a few weeks before a competition. This loss is made up naturally in 1 - 2 weeks. On the day before the competition, the martial artist's own blood is transfused back in, artificially increasing the haemoglobin level.

This can be dangerous because it increases the heart's work-load. It also upsets the body's blood-producing systems and can lead to anaemia.

RESPIRATORY CONDITIONS AFFECTING TRAINING

Asthma is a common allergic disease during which the muscles of the bronchi go into spasm making it difficult for the sufferer to breathe out. The lungs fill with air and new air cannot be drawn in, causing a feeling of suffocation or actual oxygen lack. One form of asthma is caused by exercise. The reason for this is unknown but attacks are precipitated by any form of exercise or training.

Asthma treatment comes in two forms. The first uses drugs to prevent attacks and the second uses drugs to relieve attacks. The latter are called *Bronchodilators* and they work by relaxing the bronchial muscles. They are administered by means of an aerosol spray.

Asthmatics should take a dose of bronchodilator before starting training and this will usually prevent an attack. Known asthmatics in the class must keep their inhalers near to hand. An asthma attack frightens both sufferer and spectator alike.

Anaemia is a condition in which the level of haemoglobin in the blood is low. This can come about through:

☐ blood loss - failure to make new blood efficiently

☐ increased rate of blood destruction.

A man is said to be anaemic when his haemoglobin level falls to below 12 grammes per 100 mls of blood. With women the figure is slightly less.

All normal people lose a small amount of blood, and hence iron, each day. In women this becomes obvious during menstruation, but everyone loses some from minor injury, or through the urine and faeces. The average life of an RBC is only 120 days. After this, they are broken down and their aminoacids go into the pool, but some of the minerals, such as iron, are not so efficiently re-cycled.

Iron-loss anaemia occurs when these losses are greater than the amount of iron taken in with the diet. This occurs in women and especially adolescent girls, when menstrual periods are too long and/or too heavy. Minor but persistent blood loss from a stomach ulcer, or from piles (*Haemorrhoids*) can occur without being noticed, and can also cause anaemia. As it develops so slowly, this anaemia can become quite severe before it produces symptoms.

RBCs are constantly being manufactured but when this process is not carried on efficiently, anaemia develops. A poor diet may contain insufficient iron, though this is very uncommon. Some people do not absorb enough iron through their intestine and so must take a diet with a higher iron content to maintain proper blood levels.

Vitamins B6 and B12 are essential to the manufacture of RBCs. A poor diet may be low in B6, and this causes anaemia. The disease known as 'Pernicious Anaemia' produces its effect by preventing

B12 from being changed into a form which the body can use.

There are several diseases which cause excessive blood destruction. Some are related to the immune system and lead to the body destroying large numbers of its RBCs through what is called 'Auto-immunity'. There are two others of importance. The first is called 'Sickle Cell Anaemia'. This occurs in people of Afro-Caribbean descent and is so named because under a microscope, the RBCs look sickle shaped. This happens because one of the aminoacids in the protein part of the haemoglobin is not what it should be.

Anaemia is caused when these odd shaped RBCs sometimes become stuck in narrow blood vessels. They then clump together and have to be destroyed.

Thallassaemia is a disease which originally came from the Mediterranean area but is now widespread as a result of the migration of populations. It is also caused by an abnormality in the haemoglobin, but in this case the body has difficulty in making some proteins.

Both diseases are inherited and only occur when both parents have the appropriate genes.

Martial artists suffering from sickle cell anaemia, or from thalassaemia may be accepted into training but they should be watched closely for signs of anaemia developing.

Haemophilia is the commonest of the blood clotting deficiency diseases. Several 'Factors' in the blood are responsible for blood clotting and a deficiency in any one of them can lead to persistent and sometimes uncontrollable bleeding. This can occur after only trivial injury and bleeding can often be into joints. If it occurs inside the skull, the result is usually death.

•

BLOOD CLOTTING DEFICIENCY DISEASES ARE AN ABSOLUTE BAR TO PRACTISING THE MARTIAL ARTS!

•

Chapter 3
CIRCULATION

CIRCULATION

We now have both nutrients and oxygen in the blood and these must be transported to the tissues. At the same time, waste products must be removed before they clog things up. This is the function of the circulatory system, the parts of which are:
□ the heart
□ the arteries
□ the capillaries
□ the blood vessels
□ the veins.

THE HEART

The heart is a highly efficient pump. It is also very reliable, which is just as well because if it wasn't, you would die! It beats about 70 times per minute for 70 - 80 years with only the minimum of routine maintenance. Those of you who wish to, can now calculate the total number of beats in a lifetime.

The heart is situated almost centrally inside the chest, just behind the lower end of the breast bone. At each side lie the lungs and behind it are the tube which takes food from the mouth to the stomach (the *Oesophagus*) and the spine.

The heart is made almost entirely of muscle and it is covered by a lubricating membrane known as the *Pericardium*. This allows it to expand and contract without friction. The heart muscle has a smooth lining which allows blood to slide easily over it.

The heart pump is divided into left and right sides by the *Septum*. This is the bit which sometimes has a hole in it. Each half of the heart has a different function. The left half receives used blood from the body. This is rich in nutrients and carbon dioxide but poor in oxygen. It is pumped to the lungs and returns from there to the right side of the heart in an oxygenated state. From there it is pumped out into the body (*Fig.13*).

Since the right side of the heart pumps only to the lungs, its muscle is not as thick as that of the left side, where blood is pumped all over the body - a considerable distance.

Each of the two halves of the heart consist of two chambers, the upper called the *Atrium* and the lower, the *Ventricle*. Each atrium receives blood from a large vein and pumps it via a non-return valve, to the ventricle. From there it is pumped out through a second set of non-return valves into the two major arteries.

A single heart beat consists of two parts, the first being a resting phase (*Diastole*) and the second being a phase of muscular contraction (the *Systole*). It is during the diastole that the atria and ventricles fill with blood. During systole, the atria contract, closing off the venous inlets and driving the blood each contains, into the ventricles. These then contract, pushing the blood out of the heart and into the general circulation.

At a resting pulse rate of 75 beats per minute, each individual beat takes 0.8 of a second, of which time 0.53 seconds is the resting phase and 0.27 seconds is the contracting phase. Each contraction pumps 70 - 90 mls of blood into the circulation, leaving about 50 mls of blood in the ventricles.

For the heart to pump efficiently, the timing of the contractions must be accurate. This is accomplished by the heart's own natural

Fig. 13
The heart

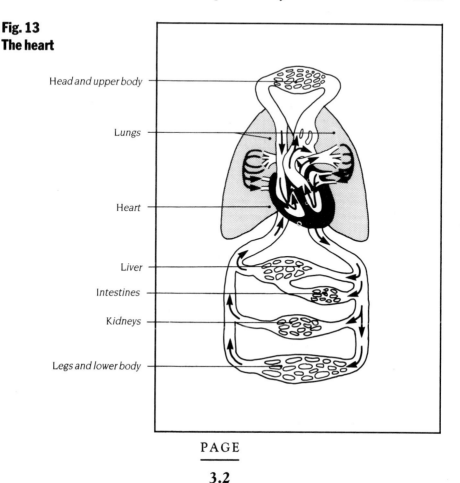

Head and upper body

Lungs

Heart

Liver

Intestines

Kidneys

Legs and lower body

'Pacemaker' which is situated in a small area of very excitable tissue known as a *Node*. The node is located high in the right atrium, near the entrance of its large vein (the *Vena cava*). The node sends out a nervous impulse spontaneously and at regular intervals, causing a wave of excitation to pass across the right and then the left atria. This excitation stimulates a contraction of those parts.

The excitation wave eventually reaches a second node, located in the left side of the heart just above the septum separating the two ventricles. It is quickly conducted from there, along bundles of specialised tissue to the apex of the ventricles. The atria and ventricles are separated by a ring of fibrous tissue and so the only route the excitation can take is through this in bundles of special tissue. From the apex, the excitation wave spreads back up through the ventricular muscle, producing a contraction.

The rate at which the heart beats is affected by:

- an increase in temperature such as during a fever,produces an increased heart rate
- drugs, some of which slow the heart rate
- nervous stimulation of the nerves of the heart will either slow the pulse rate, or quicken it
- breathing also affects heart rate and during inspiration, the heart rate increases. Heart rate returns to normal during expiration. This is the *Sinus rhythm* and it is entirely normal.

BLOOD VESSELS

As I mentioned earlier in this chapter, there are three types of blood vessel, the artery, the capillary and the vein. The *Pulmonary artery* comes from the right ventricle and takes de-oxygenated blood to the lungs. The *Aorta* comes from the left ventricle, and delivers blood to the rest of the body.

The aorta divides into large arteries which supply blood to the head, the limbs and to each of the internal organs such as the kidneys, liver, stomach. Arteries divide into smaller and smaller branches, the smallest being called *Arterioles*.

The arterioles ultimately divide into the *Capillaries*. These have an internal diameter roughly the same as an RBC. The walls are very thin, being composed of a single layer of cells. This makes it easy for fluid to pass from plasma to interstitial fluid and back again. It also allows WBCs to migrate from the capillaries when necessary.

Within two seconds of it entering a capillary, the blood has given up its supply of nutrients and oxygen, whilst at the same time taking up waste products. Capillaries join together to form the smallest veins (*Venules*) and these subsequently join together to produce veins until they finally form the *Vena cava* which returns blood to the right atrium of the heart. The pulmonary artery follows a similar sequence before returning blood to the left atrium of the heart through the pulmonary vein.

A complete circuit therefore looks like *Fig. 14*

Arteries are made up of three layers of tissue:
- an outer protective layer of fibrous tissue
- a thick layer of muscle
- a smooth lining.

Fig. 14
Blood circulation through the body

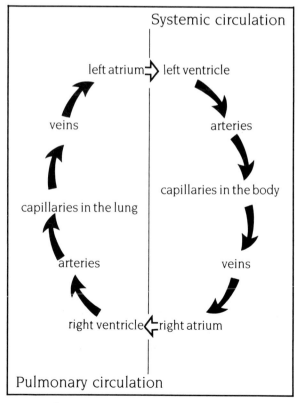

Systemic circulation

left atrium → left ventricle

veins   arteries

capillaries in the lung   capillaries in the body

arteries   veins

right ventricle ← right atrium

Pulmonary circulation

Arteries are elastic and stretch with each heart beat. This can be detected as the 'Pulse' in various parts of the body. Arterial walls contain many nerve endings called 'Stretch receptors'. These sense the pressure inside the artery.

Blood is pumped under pressure into the arterial system, and this is controlled by the muscles within the arterial walls. This pressure is eventually dissipated in the net of capillaries. Blood pressure ('B.P.') is conventionally measured in terms of the pressure exerted by a column of mercury whose height is expressed in millimetres.

Arterial blood pressure measured during contraction (the systolic B.P.) is normally about 120 mms and during diastole, this falls to 70 mms. This would normally be written as 120/70. Pressure is constant through the arteries but it drops rapidly in the arterioles and capillaries so that by the time it reaches the veins, it is only about 100 mms of pressure. This level of pressure is necessary to pump blood through all the body's blood vessels, often against the resistance of the muscular arterial walls. These respond to the stretch receptors and by contracting, they ensure that the blood pressure is constant, whether it be at the top of the head, or at the feet. The arteries also adjust the blood pressure during changes of posture, such as going from a standing to a sitting position.

Blood pressure can increase as a result of increased heart output, or through increased arterial resistance. The former can be due to emotions such as anger or excitement, the latter to drugs, some diseases, or to hardening of the arteries (*Arterio-sclerosis*).

Because blood entering the venous system is under low pressure, vein walls tend to be thin and contain little muscle (*Fig. 15*). In fact blood is pumped back to the heart entirely by the squeezing action of muscles in the tissues through which the veins pass. To prevent a backwards flow of blood, the veins have frequent non-return valves in them. The results of failure in these one-way systems can be seen in persons suffering from varicose veins.

The amount of blood that is pumped through the body (the 'Cardiac output') is the product of the amount of blood pumped out at each contraction (the 'Stroke volume') multiplied by the heart rate. With a resting pulse rate of 60 beats per minute, the amount of blood pumped with each contraction is approximately 80 mls, so the cardiac output is 4.8 litres per minute. During exercise, an increased volume of venous blood is returned to the heart and this, plus nervous stimulation, results in an increased heart rate. If the heart rate rises to 200 beats per minute, then cardiac output increases to 16 litres per minute.

The rate at which the heart fills puts a top limit on the maximum heart rate. As I have already mentioned, the resting diastole takes 0.53 seconds. Compare this with only 0.14 seconds available for fil-ling when the heart is beating at 200 beats/minute. In theory the heart can beat at about 400 times per minute but in practice, the maximum rate is around 230 beats/minute.

As the heart rate accelerates to 400% above the resting state, more blood is needed in the active circulation. The ventricles contract with greater force and less is left behind after each stroke. The blood which pools in the abdominal veins must be brought

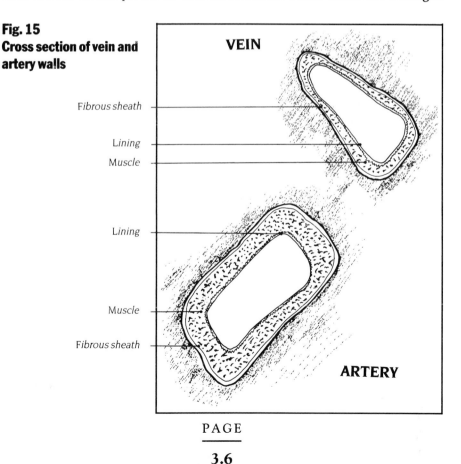

Fig. 15
Cross section of vein and artery walls

Fibrous sheath

Lining

Muscle

Lining

Muscle

Fibrous sheath

VEIN

ARTERY

into the general circulation. A large volume of blood is used by the digestive system, so this must be diverted to the muscles. It is for this reason that no strenuous exercise should be undertaken within two hours of a meal. Ignoring this advice will result in either the stomach or the muscles being starved of blood.

EFFECTS OF TRAINING

Though the heart is a muscle, it does not respond to training in exactly the same way as the muscles of the skeleton. The mechanics of what are termed *Aerobic* and *Anaerobic* respiration of muscle are dealt with in the following chapter but suffice it to say for now that heart muscle has little or no anaerobic capacity and so all training concerning the heart is aerobic in nature.

As with the training of any body system, the heart responds to being worked at a higher rate than usual by increasing its efficiency. The heart is less efficient when it works at maximum practical speed because it does not have time to fill properly. Instead, it works most efficiently at 80% of maximum, which in most people corresponds to a rate of around 170 beats/minute. This is the usual level recommended as being sustainable over long periods.

However, as one passes the 20th birthday mark, the blood vessels gradually become less elastic and less responsive to the demands made upon them. Therefore the maximum sustainable heart rate reduces for any age above 20, and is given by the formula:

190 − age = maximum sustainable heart rate

So for a 40 year old, the maximum sustainable rate is:

190 − 40 = 150 beats/minute

Training affects both the heart rate and the stroke volume but it cannot shorten the time taken to fill the heart with blood. Whereas the resting heart rate of an untrained person would typically lie between 60 - 80 beats/minute, that of the trained person drops to 40 - 50. The reason for this happening is that the heart's capacity actually increases, so each contraction pumps out a larger quantity of blood and fewer beats are necessary to maintain the resting cardiac output.

Increase in capacity occurs because the muscle fibres in the heart get longer and thicker, so they can produce more power. This makes the heart both heavier and larger. The heart of an average person may weight 300 grammes, whereas that of a trained martial artist of similar size may weigh anything up to 500 grammes. These figures, it should be mentioned, apply to men. The amount of blood remaining in the ventricles after contraction increases from 50 mls to over 100 mls.

The nett result of all this adaptation is that the maximum cardiac output increases from 16 litres/minute to 20 - 30 litres/minute. To cope with this increased flow, blood supply to the heart increases and up to 50% more capillaries open up in the muscle. Remember that a cardiac output of 20 litres per minute requires a venous return of like quantity.

When training begins, increased muscular activity pumps more venous blood to the heart, so extra supplies are on hand to match the increased cardiac output. When exercise finishes, the heart does not instantly change from its high-output phase of 20 litres/minute to its resting state of only 5 litres/minute. On the other hand, if the muscles stop pumping blood back to the heart, the heart quickly runs out of blood to pump and this causes a dramatic fall in blood pressure. The martial artist who suddenly stops after intensive training will often feel faint and may even pass out! This is an important reason for an active 'warming down' period following any training.

HEART ABNORMALITIES
There are two types of cardiac abnormalities:
□ congenital abnormalities which occur during the development of the heart before birth
□ acquired abnormalities arising out of disease or degeneration.

Congenital abnormalities are either anatomical, or they are functional. An example of an anatomical congenital abnormality is a defective septum, separating the two ventricles. This is commonly known as a 'Hole in the heart'. The actual hole itself can vary in size from a pinhead, to a total absence - in which case the heart has in effect, only 1 ventricle. This allows arterial and venous blood to mix, so the circulating blood contains less oxygen than normal.

A second example of anatomical congenital abnormality affects the heart valves. These can be too small - in which the case the heart must work harder at any particular level of output - or they may be incorrectly formed, so they cannot withstand the pressures put on them. Sometimes the valves are in the wrong place!

These abnormalities can occur separately, or in any combination but fortunately they can now be dealt with satisfactorily through surgery. This however, may not mean that the heart becomes normal; only that it is better than it was before.

Incidentally, people who undergo heart surgery have to take drugs to slow blood clotting. These drugs make them bleed more easily and is an *absolute* bar to practising the martial arts.

Congenital functional abnormalities occur in the origin and conducting of the heart beat, so the heart beats in a disorganised and inefficient way. These abnormalities sometimes appear on their own, but are otherwise seen as part of other inherited disorders.

Heart muscle is sometimes over-excitable and this results in a very rapid heart rate felt as 'Palpitations'. These lead to dizziness and poor filling of the heart.

Acquired cardiac abnormalities result from illnesses and they can be either acute (having severe symptoms and a short course), or chronic (persisting for a long time). The acute form can arise through inflammation of the heart muscle following a virus infection. The only outward sign of this may be an influenza-type illness. In these circumstances, over-stimulation of the heart as a result of training or competition can actually lead to cardiac arrest and death!

This is not uncommon, so beware! It is unwise for anyone to train hard, or to compete within 3-4 weeks after a viral illness.

Chronic heart disease may affect the valves, and this is seen in the case of childhood Rheumatic fever. Thankfully it is now not so common. Much more common is disease resulting from a reduced blood supply to the heart muscle.

The most spectacular (if that is the word) form of this is the heart attack - a *Coronary thrombosis*. One of the arteries becomes blocked by a blood clot and the heart muscle it supplies then dies. A coronary thrombosis occurs when the lining of the artery is damaged by arterio-sclerosis (*see page 3.5*) and it is usually made worse by a spasm of the affected artery, causing a total blockage.

Spasm of the artery can occur of itself, without a clot being present and if this is not quickly relieved (spontaneously or otherwise), the result is the same and some heart muscle dies.

The dead heart muscle is eventually absorbed, and the defect repaired by strong fibrous tissue. However, the resulting scar can act as an over-excitable focus and cause irregular beats.

When the heart is beating both strongly and quickly, the smaller blood vessels which supply the heart muscle become squeezed, so blood supply is reduced. It is only during the diastole that a full supply gets through to the muscle. It therefore follows that if the blood supply is already deficient, this further reduction can be of vital importance.

The heart has an enormous reserve of capacity above and beyond that needed in everyday life. It is this reserve which is reduced as a result of a heart attack. Actually, the heart has very good and reliable safety mechanisms which begin to operate well before the stage of further damage is reached. These safety mechanisms reveal themselves in the form of:

□ shortness of breath
□ pain.

Everyone breathes more rapidly during exercise and when this reaches a stage where not enough air can be taken in, the limit has been reached. A normal heart can cope with a certain amount of this but a damaged one cannot.

Pain which originates from the heart is known as *Angina*. It is very specific and these are its characteristics:

□ it only appears with exercise
□ it is very regular insofar as it always requires the same level of exertion to bring it on
□ it is centred in the middle of the chest, at the lower end of the breastbone
□ it is described as feeling like a tight band around the chest
□ it may radiate to the shoulders and upper arms, particularly on the left side
□ it goes away after resting.

Angina is caused by an insufficient blood supply to the heart muscle, so not enough oxygen is supplied and waste products are not removed quickly enough. Angina should not be ignored. When it comes on, training should stop and the individual must rest at least until all the symptoms have gone away.

All safety mechanisms can be over-ridden - either consciously or subconsciously - and there are always people who will attempt to do more than they are capable of. If they are physically normal, then little harm will be done but this does not apply where there is heart damage. Sufferers must keep within their own limitations as demonstrated by chest pain and/or breathlessness.

Beware over-riding these safety mechanisms subconsciously, such as during gradings or competitions.

So far, I have spoken about only the ill-effects of exercise upon the less than perfect heart. There are however, many benefits to be gained from training to the limit. As I mentioned before, training increases the size and strength of heart muscle and most importantly, it opens up many more capillaries which improve blood supply to the heart itself. All of these will help a person suffering from a heart condition to cope much better with the demands of everyday living.

Cardiac arrest means that the heart stops beating effectively. Nothing happens for 15 - 30 seconds, then the victim becomes unconscious and often experiences what looks like a fit. Two minutes after the heart stops beating, the brain is irreversibly damaged and after four minutes, the heart is most unlikely to re-start. There are two reasons for the heart suddenly stopping:
□ vagal inhibition
□ ventricular fibrillation
Left to its own devices, the heart would operate at a rate of around 100 beats per minute. The function of a nerve called the *Vagus* is to slow the heart, so it beats at a more normal rate. If however, the vagus is over-stimulated, the heart can actually stop altogether, either for a few seconds only, or permanently.

Vagal inhibition can occur in several circumstances and is always more likely if the victim is stressed up, tense or excited, such as during a competition or grading. Inhibition can be caused by a hard blow to the lower part of the chest, by pressure on the neck (down which the vagus passes), or by a sudden shock. The shock can be physical as would happen if you fell into icy water, or it could be emotional - such as being literally frightened to death.

Ventricular fibrillation is a condition in which the heart beat is completely uncontrolled and very rapid, sometimes reaching 400+ beats/minute. Strictly speaking of course, this is not a cardiac arrest, though the effects are identical, and the heart will in any case stop after 4 - 5 minutes if the condition is left untreated.

Ventricular fibrillation may be caused by patches of over-excitable or irritated tissue in the ventricular muscle. These sometimes occur in the presence of scar tissue resulting from a coronary thrombosis, or they may be stimulated during periods of angina.

Cardiac arrest is by no means unknown in the training or competition area and this is why there should always be at least one person trained in resuscitation techniques present. It is also a reason why no-one who has had heart trouble should be allowed in competition.

All martial artists who have had heart trouble must heed the warning symptoms and additionally, they must warm down properly after training to avoid unnecessary strain on the the heart.

Abnormally high blood pressure (*Hypertension*) is associated with some diseases, notably those of the kidney. In older people, it can also be caused by arterio-sclerosis. In both cases, high blood pressure occurs when there is an increase in the resistance of blood flow through the circulatory system.

As the cardiac output increases during training, the normal person compensates by relaxing the arteries and therefore lowering peripheral resistance to blood flow. This will maintain a reasonable but still slightly elevated blood pressure. The person suffering from hypertension does not have this degree of compensation and blood pressure can therefore rise to catastrophic levels.

People who suffer from hypertension must be very careful when training, so this situation does not arise.

From the coach's point of view, it is most important that applicants with a history of heart trouble are referred to their doctors. Sometimes a simple medical examination will reveal whether the heart can cope with training. Occasionally a stress test is necessary. This measures the heart's performance as it is exercised to, or above its limit. The stress test must be done only in facilities which have resuscitation equipment to hand.

Chapter 4
MUSCLES

Muscles are the 'engines' by which all movement is produced. Three types of muscle are found in the body:
☐ skeletal (or striated)
☐ cardiac
☐ smooth.

Cardiac muscle has already been described in the previous chapter and smooth muscle is that which occurs in such internal organs as the lungs and the intestines - so it is not relevant to this book.

Skeletal muscle produces all voluntary movement (*Fig. 16*). Individual skeletal muscles come in all shapes and sizes, being variously cylindrical, spindle shaped, strap shaped, fan shaped etc. They can vary in size from 25 millimetres (as in the case of an eye muscle), to 600 millimetres (as in the thigh muscle). Nevertheless they are all made in the same way, and consist of:
☐ a fibrous sheath
☐ tendons
☐ the muscle belly.

The fibrous sheath is necessary to keep the muscle in shape and if it is cut, the muscle belly protrudes and force of contraction is weakened. Tendons attach muscles to the parts to be moved. Usually these are bones but such muscles as those of the face attach to skin only and make it possible to look fierce, or to purse the lips as the occasion warrants.

Each muscle has a point of origin and another of insertion. The former is relatively stationary and the latter is the bit that moves.

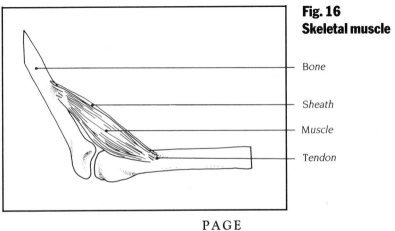

Fig. 16
Skeletal muscle

Bone

Sheath

Muscle

Tendon

Occasionally however, these are reversible, as in the case of the muscles which pull the foot up. These will also pull the leg down if the foot is fixed, such as during standing.

The muscle belly is the part which does all the contracting, for muscles can only pull - they cannot push. Each muscle is made up of numerous bundles, each of which contains about 50 fibres (*Fig. 17*). The muscle fibre is a single cell, being very long in relation to its diameter in the ratio of about 500:1. The longest muscle fibres of all are found in the thigh, where they reach lengths of about 50 millimetres. Each muscle fibre consists of a number of parts, the most important of which are:

□ fibrils
□ mitochondria
□ glycogen
□ myoglobin

The fibrils are the parts of the muscle which do all the contracting. When examined under a microscope, they are seen to have stripes, or striations running across them, and these give the muscle its alternative name. The stripes are actually parallel rows of a very heavy protein called myosin. Between them and free to slide in and out are filaments of a much lighter protein called *Actin* (*Fig. 18*).

When the muscle fibre is stimulated by a nerve, these proteins attract each other and the actin filaments slide between the myosin, shortening the fibril by about 30%. When the fibre contracts, it does so on an 'all-or-nothing' basis. This means that

Fig. 17
Structure of muscle

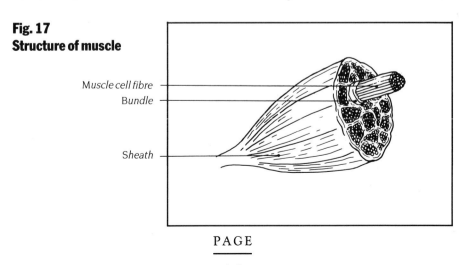

Muscle cell fibre
Bundle

Sheath

during most movements, only a part of the muscle is active, the rest takes no part. It is only when maximum strength is being applied that all the cells in a muscle are used.

Every cell in the body contains *Mitochondria*. These are sausage shaped miniature chemical factories which produce all the energy needed by the cell. They are particularly numerous in muscle fibres, where there is a high energy requirement.

Glycogen has been previously mentioned in Chapter 1 (see page 1.3). It is the muscle cell's instantly available store of fuel and is quickly converted to glucose when the need arises. Myoglobin holds the muscle's reserve supply of oxygen. It takes up oxygen in the same way as does haemoglobin in the blood, and only gives it back up when the amount reaching the muscle falls to a very low level.

Three types of striated muscle fibre have been identified on the basis of their capacity for aerobic respiration and speed of contraction. They are called:
□ fast twitch white fibres
□ fast twitch yellow fibres
□ slow twitch red fibres

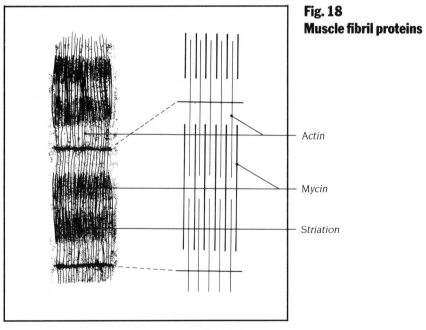

Fig. 18
Muscle fibril proteins

Actin

Mycin

Striation

All three types are found in striated muscle, but in different proportions. Additionally, the proportions of slow to fast twitch fibres varies between individuals. This is the reason why all sports are not suitable for all people. Slow twitch red muscle fibres have the greatest capacity for aerobic respiration whilst fast twitch white fibres have more anaerobic capacity. The yellow fibres are intermediate between the two.

Greatest concentrations of slow twitch fibres are found in skeletal muscles which are constantly active, such as those concerned with respiration and posture-maintenance. They seem to contain more mitochondria and myoglobin than the fast twitch fibres.

INTERNAL RESPIRATION OF MUSCLE

We have previously seen how food is digested by the body, and how the circulation takes nutrients to all parts of the body. We now examine what happens to the food inside the muscle cell.

Adenosine triphosphate is a chemical compound present in the cell. As its name implies, it is made up of a substance called *Adenosine*, to which three phosphate groups are strongly attached. When one of the phosphate bonds to the adenosine is broken, a lot of energy is released and *Adenosine diphosphate* and phosphoric acid are formed. If a second bond is broken, yet more energy is released and *Adenosine monophosphate* plus additional phosphoric acid results.

This process takes place with the help of water and for this reason, it is named *Hydrolysis*. It is reversible insofar as if energy is put into the system, adenosine monophosphate is successively converted back to adenosine diphosphate and then adenosine triphosphate.

This can be represented as follows:

$$A*P\text{-}P\text{-}P + ENERGY \lozenge A*P\text{-}P + ENERGY + P \lozenge A*P + ENERGY + P$$
        (ATP)   (ADP)   (AMP)

: where A is adenosine and P is phosphoric acid.

The energy released by this process is used by the muscle to produce a contraction. There is only enough ATP in each cell to maintain a contraction for a very short time (of the order of less than 1 second, in fact). Nevertheless its concentration in the cell remains the same no matter how hard the training and it only falls when the point of exhaustion is reached.

Levels of ATP are maintained in the cell by 3 systems. These are:
☐ the aerobic system
☐ the anaerobic system
☐ the phosphocreatine system.

The aerobic system is so named because it uses oxygen and glucose to produce ATP. Both of these are supplied to the cell by the interstitial fluid which in turn receives them from the blood. First of all the glucose is broken down in a complex series of chemical actions that leads to a substance known as *Pyruvic acid*. During this process, enough energy is produced to convert 9 units of ADP to energy-rich ATP. In the next phase, oxygen is used to break the pyruvic acid down in stages, to carbon dioxide and water. This phase converts a further 30 units of ADP to ATP, so expressed in nett terms, 1 unit of glucose rebuilds 39 units of ATP.

The chemical reactions involved in these processes take place in the mitochondria and are dependent upon an adequate supply of oxygen. When this is not available, the anaerobic cycle comes into operation.

The anaerobic system operates without oxygen. The starting place is the glycogen store in the muscle fibre itself. This is converted to glucose, and then broken down to pyruvic acid. From this point onwards, the aerobic and anaerobic cycles operate differently. In the anaerobic system, the pyruvic acid is broken down in the absence of oxygen to a waste product called *Lactic acid*.

Lactic acid diffuses into the interstitial fluid and reaches the bloodstream, where it is soaked up by the buffering system mentioned on page 2.7. Some of it is taken up by the liver, and some is used as fuel by the heart muscle. The majority remains in the blood. In the presence of oxygen, lactic acid is reconverted first to pyruvic acid and then to carbon dioxide and water.

When there is no buffering capacity left in the blood, lactic acid begins to accumulate in the muscle. This makes the intracellular fluid too acid, so the muscle stops working. The result is very painful muscular exhaustion. The body is said to have incurred an 'Oxygen debt' and like all debts, this must be repaid as soon as possible. 'Repayment' is made by the heart and breathing rates remaining higher than they normally would in the resting state, and by this means a surplus of oxygen is taken to the tissues.

The accumulation of lactic acid in the muscles is a further reason for going through an effective warm-down session after training. It keeps the muscles and circulation active, so lactic acid is washed out of the tissues as rapidly as possible.

Anaerobic respiration is less fuel efficient in that each unit of glucose only re-converts 3 units of ATP. This makes it only one thirteenth as efficient as the aerobic process. Even so, anaerobic respiration represents a big reserve of energy because large quantities of glycogen are stored in the muscle.

Muscles can start working at full capacity upon demand. A martial artist begins training at a pace which he knows he can maintain for the whole session (i.e., under aerobic conditions). His heart and respiration rates do not immediately switch into high gear and so there is initially nothing to convert ADP back to ATP. This means he would quickly become exhausted were it not for the *Phosphocreatine* ('PC') system.

Phosphocreatine is a compound consisting of creatine and one phosphate group. The phosphate group is easily shed and made available to reform ATP. If the system is used on its own, it provides sufficient reserves of PC for 9 - 10 seconds. Once used up, PC is not reformed until some spare oxygen becomes available. Therefore using the phosphocreatine energy system causes an oxygen debt and it is when this is repaid that the martial artist gets his second wind.

Just because three respiratory systems are available does not mean that they are used individually. The PC system starts the process going but this is quickly taken over by the anaerobic and aerobic processes. The aerobic system is the basic one and this is added to as necessary by the anaerobic system. These two systems usually work together and on occasion, all three might well operate at the same time.

Different activities make different demands on the internal respiratory systems. Intense but short lived activity of around 10 seconds' duration relies heavily on the phosphocreatine system. Heavy exertion lasting up to two minutes will mostly use the anaerobic system. Longer training at lower intensities uses the aerobic process. Martial art practice includes all of these.

AEROBIC TRAINING

A good aerobic capacity is the basis for good health in the martial artist and, for that matter, in anyone else. Firstly, the longer the muscles can work under aerobic conditions, the less the fatigue-producing anaerobic system will be needed. Secondly, the more efficient the aerobic system, the more quickly used anaerobic capacity can be restored when the training has ended.

As I mentioned in the section dealing with the heart, one effect of aerobic training is to open up larger numbers of capillaries in the muscle. In fact, the muscle of a highly trained martial artist may show as many as 100 times more capillaries as the muscle of a poorly trained one. This huge increase speeds up the passage of glucose and oxygen from blood to muscle fibre, and also the return flow of waste products out of the muscle. This happens because they do not have so far to diffuse through the interstitial fluid.

Aerobic training also increases the number and size of the cell's chemical factories - the mitochondria. This allows them to process larger quantities of glucose, glycogen, pyruvic acid and oxygen. Additionally, the muscle's store of ready-use materials increases greatly and this improves the muscle's capacity for work. However, it does seem as though the level of ATP in the cell is not measurably increased.

Bear in mind that aerobic training does not have an effect on all muscles. Only those which are worked constantly to their aerobic limits will show the changes mentioned above. Therefore the martial artist must exercise the whole of his body in an aerobic fashion and this can be done by combining running with punching and kicking activities over a period of 10 minutes or so. Intensity of work should be kept below maximum so anaerobic capacity is not eaten into.

Aerobic capacity is quite easy to monitor and this can be done by the martial artist himself, or by the coach. It depends upon working over a fixed period of perhaps 10 - 12 minutes at a heart rate of around 170 beats/minute (or at its age-related level, *see page 3.7*). At the end of the session, the heart is counted for 15 seconds in every 30 seconds until it returns to its resting level. The length of time this takes is a measure of the aerobic fitness and a good recovery time is about 90 seconds.

Another way to measure fitness is to time a run of 2 miles or so whilst holding a heart rate of 170 beats/minute. As aerobic fitness improves, the time gets shorter.

It is not always necessary to to physically count the pulse, which is just as well because this can be rather inconvenient, especially if it involves stopping training. With experience, the martial artist will soon come to recognise the particular sensations in the breathing and in the muscles which are associated with this steady-state exercise.

Do note that the above are measurements of improvement only and when improvement ceases, the martial artist has become as aerobically fit as it is possible for him to be. Note also that the results of these measurements apply to individuals only, and not to groups of students. With this very much in mind, the same methods can be applied but with suitable modifications to both the healthy 18 year old and to the student who has just recovered from a heart attack.

ANAEROBIC TRAINING

Anaerobic capacity does not depend upon the muscle's supply of glycogen and myoglobin because there is more than enough of these in the tissue; it is related entirely to the fate of lactic acid. Anaerobic capacity is exhausted when so much lactic acid has built up in the muscle, that it is prevented from working.

Training affects anaerobic capacity in the following three ways:
☐ there is an increased uptake of lactic acid by the liver
☐ there is an increase in the usage of lactic acid as fuel
  by the heart
☐ there is a more rapid diffusion of lactic acid from muscle fibre
  into the blood. To some extent, of course, this is due to the
  increase in blood supply resulting from aerobic training.

These improvements are achieved by working the system repeatedly and to its limit. In the case of anaerobic training, this means hard work performed over a period of 2 minutes or so, followed by an active rest period of 5 -10 minutes. The rest period allows the aerobic system to regenerate the anaerobic process. Following the rest, hard work is resumed.

As a practical example of what I mean, the martial artist might perform press-ups or squat-thrusts at near maximum effort, so the muscles become exhausted in less than 2 minutes. This is then followed by 5 - 6 minutes of jogging, or an equivalent exercise.

There is no accurate method for measuring improvement in anaerobic capacity. A laboratory can measure the amounts of lactic acid in the blood and in the muscles but the only way to achieve it in the training hall is by noting that little Willie can now keep up his squat thrusts for 90 seconds instead of the 60 seconds which he did last month.

PHOSPHOCREATINE SYSTEM

When used alone, this system exhausts itself in 5 - 10 seconds. The object in training is use up all the PC without producing lots of lactic acid. One way of achieving this might be to shadow-spar at maximum effort for 10 seconds, followed by 2 - 3 minutes of light sparring, so the aerobic processes can rebuild PC ready for the next interval of hard effort. The same results could be achieved in the training hall by such exercises as relay-racing.

As you can probably tell from all this, achieving maximum aerobic/anaerobic health is a time-consuming process which can eat into several hours of each day. This is perhaps justifiable only if the martial artist is totally dedicated to his art, or wishes to compete internationally. Certainly, the average student has other things to occupy his/her time, such as earning a living, or chasing the current girl/boy friend.

Nevertheless these principles still apply and can be altered and adapted to suit the interests and aptitudes of any particular individual or class. In the final analysis, it is up to the coach to balance the achievement and entertainment value of his training, with the attitudes of the students taught.

MUSCLE TONE

All muscles have what is called 'Tone'. This is a constant slight state of tension and means that the muscle is actually working at a low rate, even when it is apparently at rest. There are 2 advantages to good muscle tone:

☐ there is no slack to be taken up so an active contraction

produces an immediate movement
☐ added support is given to the joints that these muscles surround. This is very important during the rehabilitation which follows injury. It is the best protection against future damage.

Muscle tone is increased by what are called *Isometric* exercises. These tighten the muscle but do not shorten its length, so that the joint to which the muscle is attached does not move. An example of an isometric neck exercise involves clasping the hands behind the head and simultaneously trying to push the head backwards while pulling the hands forwards. This isometrically exercises both the muscles pulling the head back, and the muscles pulling the arms forward.

Similar exercises can be devised for any group of muscles, pitting one set of muscles against an opposing set - as in the example just given - or by working the muscles against an immovable object such as a solid wall, or a heavy weight. It is important to remember that if one set of muscles is exercised, then those which produce the opposite movement (the Antagonists) must also be exercised. This ensures that the resting position of the joint is maintained.

Isometric exercise increases the bulk of muscle, causing each muscle fibre to grow fatter. There is no increase in the number of muscle cells. Rather, the greater thickness comes about through an increase in the contractile proteins myosin and actin within the fibrils. By this means, the muscles become stronger, since strength depends entirely upon the bulk of the muscles involved.

Isometric contractions cannot be kept up for long periods. They soon become painful as a result of a shortage of blood to the muscle. This occurs because muscular tension squeezes the capillaries and reduces blood supply.

When muscles contract to produce a movement, the antagonist muscles must stretch. To help this to happen, the antagonists lose some or all of their tone in a process called 'Relaxation'. Relaxation is therefore a reflex action, it is not normally under conscious control.

Each muscle contains large numbers of specialised fibres which, although they contract and relax in the same way as normal fibres do, they actually have very little strength. They are however, able to sense the state of contraction and the length of a muscle and their function is:

□ to sense the position of the body and limbs
□ to protect muscles and joint during movement
□ to relax antagonist muscles during a movement.

The position sense is what provides the brain with an image of where the different parts of the body are, and what they are doing. Without this sense, movements such as walking would be very inefficient, and the maintenance of balance almost impossible.

Walking and balancing have both been learned. Martial arts techniques are learned in exactly the same way, so they can be performed expertly. It seems obvious to me that they will be learned most efficiently when initially performed slowly and smoothly. This allows the sequence of sensations associated with the execution of each technique to be imprinted on the memory. The required strength and speed associated with the technique can be developed at a later stage.

Uncontrolled muscular activity will damage other muscles, tendons and joint ligaments, by over-stretching them. By sensing both the length of the muscle and the speed of movement, the stretch receptors can stimulate antagonist muscles to contract and so slow down or halt the movement before damage is caused.

This has a direct bearing upon exercising for flexibility. Bear in mind that any strong stimulation of the stretch receptors will cause a reflex muscular contraction which limits the degree of stretch attained.

Ballistic stretching exercises, such as arm swinging, or bouncing up and down on an already extended hip will only stimulate the antagonists to contract and so actually restrict the movement.

Forcible stretching also causes damage. The stretched muscle can tear, or the ligaments of the joint it protects can be damaged. In either case, flexibility will ultimately be reduced.

Such practices as assisted hip flexion (high kicking) and increasing stretch in the splits by addition of weight, should be banned.

MUSCLE INJURY
Muscles can be injured in two ways:
□ by a direct blow

□ as a result of their own action - too hard a contraction.

The injury can occur at:

□ the join between tendon and bone

□ the join between tendon and muscle

□ the middle of the tendon

□ the muscle belly.

It is a general rule that places where different tissues join together are especially susceptible to injury. This is certainly true of muscular injuries where the great majority of tears occur at the junctions of bone to tendon and muscle to tendon. A tear at these sites always results in some bleeding into the area, and this gives rise to pain and tenderness. Pain occurs if the injured part is further stretched.

While passive movement of the affected muscle is painless, active movement is painful. For example, if certain shoulder muscles are torn, the arm can easily be lifted sideways to a right angle by someone else, but an attempt to move the arm under its own power to the same position may be defeated because of the pain caused.

A tear in the middle of the tendon is not very common. This is because tendons contain elastic tissue which provides them with sufficient stretch and resilience to protect against injury. However, advancing years, or previous injury both result in the replacement of elastic tissue by ordinary fibrous tissue. This makes the tendon less resilient and more likely to be injured.

The two most common tendon ruptures occur at the Achilles tendon in the ankle, and at the Biceps tendon in the arm. Sometimes the Achilles tendon is only partially ruptured and slowly heals itself without the need for an operation. A complete rupture, however, will never heal on its own because muscle tone pulls the torn edges so far apart that healing is impossible.

Achilles tendon rupture is a serious injury, requiring surgery and 3 - 6 months in plaster to allow it to heal. A similar period is then required for the ankle joint to regain mobility. Even after all this, the tendon is left weaker than it was before the rupture.

This injury hardly ever occurs without warning. If certain forms of training or exercises cause pain and tenderness at the back of the ankle, then they should be completely avoided until the cause has been discovered and the condition properly treated. A 6 - 8 week lay-off from training to rest a strained Achilles tendon is much better than a 6 - 12 month lay-off to heal a ruptured one!

Rupture of the Biceps tendon occurs in older people and it is not treated by operation. Actually it results in little disability other than a rather unusual lump caused by the muscle contracting without resistance.

Injury to the belly of the muscle is caused either by a blow on the muscle (usually when it is contracted), or by a powerful contraction which tears muscle tissue. A blow on the muscle ruptures blood vessels, so bleeding into the muscle tissue occurs. Blood is a very irritating fluid when outside of a blood vessel and its presence in the tissues causes pain and unpleasant muscle spasm.

A deficit in the smooth outline of the muscle can indicate where muscle tissue is actually torn. This also results in a lot of bleeding and similar effects to that described previously. Muscle tears arising out of powerful contractions are more likely to happen when there has been previous damage.

In both types of injury, the repair process follows the usual pattern of absorbtion of blood and dead tissue, and then a gluing together of the healthy tissues. The injury is finally strengthened with fibrous tissue. All this takes 3-12 weeks, depending upon the extent of the damage. A torn muscle benefits only rarely from being sewn up.

The speed and effectiveness of rehabilitation following injury is matched by the speed and effectiveness of the first aid applied. Ice, compression and elevation ('I.C.E.') limit the amount of bleeding and reduce pain, so the injured part can be mobilised more quickly. This is important because it prevents injured tissues from sticking to nearby ones. If this happens, dragging on the scar tissue will cause pain and limit movement.

DISEASES OF MUSCLES

Most diseases which cause malfunction of the muscles attack the nerves, and will be dealt with later. Actually, diseases of the muscle fibres themselves are not common. They are mainly congenital in origin, start from childhood or adolescence and result in progressive muscular weakness through muscle fibre degeneration. Life expectation is usually greatly reduced.

In such cases, martial art training would not affect the course of the disease for better or for worse. Whether or not anyone suffering from these diseases should be offered a chance to train in the martial arts depends upon their degree of disability at the time. However, a major factor should be whether it might improve the quality of what life is left to them.

Of more immediate importance is disease of the tendon sheath. Long tendons run in a sheath containing a lubricating fluid. This reduces friction. However, repetitive movement of the tendon over a long period may cause the sheath to become inflamed and the lubricating fluid to dry up. The result of this is pain on movement and a feeling of friction which can be detected as a crackling sensation (*Crepitus*) over the affected tendon. This condition is known as *Synovitis* and it is best treated by resting the tendon for around 3 weeks, when the inflammation will have cleared up. This is providing, of course, that the tendon has not been moved so as to cause pain.

Equally important, the action which caused the synovitis in the first place must be identified and not used in the future. Synovitis is a totally preventable condition and it only arises as a result of bad training practices.

Chapter 5
THE SKELETON

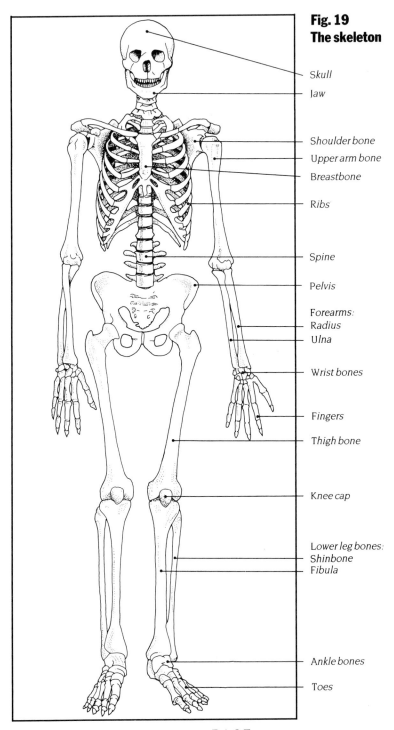

Fig. 19
The skeleton

Skull

Jaw

Shoulder bone

Upper arm bone

Breastbone

Ribs

Spine

Pelvis

Forearms:
Radius
Ulna

Wrist bones

Fingers

Thigh bone

Knee cap

Lower leg bones:
Shinbone
Fibula

Ankle bones

Toes

The skeleton is made up of bones and the joints between them (*Fig. 19*). The bones give a basic shape to the body and without them, we would be spread out on the floor like a jellyfish. Bones come in a variety of shapes, types and sizes, such as:
□ long bones
□ flat bones
□ the vertebrae.

All bones have the same structure. They are surrounded by a tough fibrous covering inside which is a layer of hard bone known as the *Cortex*. This contains the mineral Calcium, which is respons-ible for giving bone its strength. Inside the cortex is a spongy substance known as the 'Marrow'. This is a honeycomb of fibrous tissue containing fat, blood vessels and blood cells.

The long bones are found in the arms, legs and ribs. They are concerned with movement and so have many muscle attachments (*Fig. 20*). Flat bones are found in the shoulder blade, the breast bone and the bones of the pelvis. The skull is largely made up of flat bones joined to form a protective box enclosing the brain. Flat

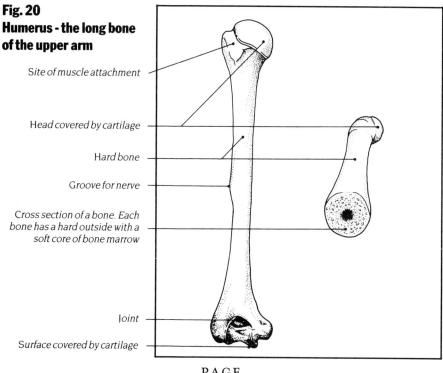

Fig. 20
Humerus - the long bone of the upper arm

Site of muscle attachment

Head covered by cartilage

Hard bone

Groove for nerve

Cross section of a bone. Each bone has a hard outside with a soft core of bone marrow

Joint

Surface covered by cartilage

bones give shape to the body and provide a solid base from which the muscles can act to move the limbs. In adults, the marrow of these flat bones manufactures all the blood cells.

The *Vertebrae* are specialised bones which combine functions of movement with stability. They also act as shock absorbers, soaking up the forces applied to the spine through such actions as walking and running. Without this, even walking would jar the brain enough to cause a severe headache.

A joint, or 'Articulation' occurs where bones come together. If the bones are separated by cartilage, then the joint is said to be 'Cartilaginous'. A fibrous joint occurs when bones are joined by fibrous tissue. All cartilaginous joints are made in the same way. The ends of both bones are covered by elastic 'Articular' cartilage and the whole is enclosed within a fibrous and ligamentous bag. This is attached to the bones by a collar, just above and below the cartilage-covered ends. This 'Joint capsule' has a smooth lining which produces a lubricating fluid to reduce the friction of the bones moving on each other. The joint is further strengthened by bands of ligaments which lie outside of the joint capsule.

There are 2 types of joints:
□ those which allow free movement
□ those which allow little or no movement.

Then there are 3 types of moving joints, all of which are cartilaginous. These are:
□ ball-and-socket joints
□ hinge joints
□ plain joints.

The shoulder and hip are ball-and-socket joints. The ends of the upper arm bone (*Humerus*) and thigh bone (*Femur*) locate into the deep cups provided in the shoulderblade (*Scapula*) and pelvis respectively. This allows movement:
□ away from, and towards the body
□ backwards and forwards
□ rotation in either direction
□ any combination of these.

By allowing such a large range of movement, such joints are basically weak, though the hip joint does have a deep socket and well-rounded ball. Additionally, both are surrounded by strong muscles, which support them.

The elbow is a hinge joint. This is to say that the shape of the bones restricts the joint to moving in the manner of a hinge. It can either bend ('Flex'), or it can straighten ('Extend'). The elbow joint is very strong and it is additionally protected by the very mobile shoulder joint.

The fingers have plain joints in which the bones simply slide over each other. They are held together only with ligaments and their movement is totally dependent upon the shape of the bone surfaces. The knee joint is a plain joint except that it is specialised in that it has 2 strong ligaments (the *Cruciates*) inside it and these make it function like a hinge joint.

Joints with little movement can be either cartilaginous or fibrous. The bones of the skull which enclose the brain butt directly against each other, and are joined by fibrous tissue only. This allows no movement at the joints. The ribs are joined to the breastbone by means of a cartilaginous joint. The collarbones have articular cartilage, ligaments, and a joint capsule. This arrangement allows a few degrees of movement only.

MOVEMENT

Movement is produced by muscles contracting, and using the bones as levers. The point about which they move is the joint. The mechanics of movement seem simple. For example, to bend the elbow requires the muscles on the front of the upper arm to contract (*See Fig. 16*). Yet if you hold a heavy weight in your fist as you bend your elbow, you will discover that not only are the biceps contracting, but also muscles over the shoulder, on the chest, in the neck and back are too! Many other muscles which cannot be felt, are also contracting. All these are necessary to stabilise the shoulder, preventing it from being pulled out of joint. They also modify the direction of pull exerted by the primary muscles.

BONE INJURIES

Good training has little appreciable effect on the bones. Bad training, however, can have serious consequences. Poor technique or a lack of control can result in fractures.

A fracture goes through the same healing process as any other injury, except that new bone must be laid down. This requires complete rest, because any movement at the fracture site may result in the bone healing incorrectly. Treatment therefore consists of immobilising the joints above and below the fracture, usually in a plaster cast. Healing takes at least 3 months but this can extend to 12 months or more.

An equal amount of time will then have to be spent upon rehabilitation. If a joint has been unused for a time, its range of movement will be very poor but with regular usage, normal movement will be regained. During this time, serious work/training may be impossible, so the physical and financial consequences of a fracture can be quite severe.

Fractures can also result in damage to nerves or arteries. This is because nerves are sometimes in contact with the bone. Careless handling may cut the nerve against a sharp end of bone. The result is a complete loss of sensation, and paralysis of the muscles below the fracture site. This sometimes repairs itself though it can take 12 months for a nerve to grow from the upper arm to the ends of the fingers. Even then, recovery may not be complete.

Arteries can be obstructed by pressure associated with the fracture. This again, can be caused by careless handling, poor positioning of a broken limb, or by poor treatment, e.g., the plaster cast is too tight. If the artery is obstructed for more than 10 minutes, the muscle below the fracture dies and is replaced by fibrous tissue. Once this begins, no treatment is then possible and the limb becomes completely useless. The only treatment then is amputation.

Stress fractures occur as a result of bad training. They are also caused by repeated minor shocks, arising out of running on hard tarmac without sufficient cushioning in the shoes. Cracks appear in the cortex of the bone but these are so small, they cannot be seen under X-ray. If the bones are further stressed, the cracks become more numerous until one day, a quite trivial shock produces a complete fracture of the bone.

Stress fractures are most common at the shin bone (the *Tibia*), and in the bones of the feet. Stress fractures in the bones of the feet were common amongst army recruits who were encouraged to stamp their feet whilst marching. For this reason, they are still referred to as 'March fractures'.

A martial artist decides to improve his general fitness by doing some running. All seems to go well except that he notices a pain in his leg as he runs. This goes away when he stops running. Each time he runs, the pain returns, but it always stops afterwards. He dismisses it as insignificant until one day he lands a little heavily on his foot and his tibia breaks!

This fracture takes as long to heal as the other types yet if the warning symptoms are acted upon, the cracks heal completely in only 3 weeks. During this time, the martial artist must avoid any activity which causes pain in his leg. When he is recovered, he should either buy a pair of better cushioned running shoes, or he should run on soft ground.

Another injury is worthy of note because it is common to martial arts practice. This is the blood clot which forms between the fibrous sheath and the bone itself, following a hard blow. The blood clot is an excellent medium for bacteria to grow in, and if they are able to, then a serious infection called *Osteomyelitis* can develop. This leads to destruction of the affected bone and if it persists, permanent disability results. The shin bone is particularly susceptible to this sort of injury because it is only thinly covered by skin.

If a swelling over the tibia remains painful, or gets worse, then urgent medical investigation is needed.

LIGAMENTS & FLEXIBILITY

Training affects the flexibility of joints. Ultimately however, the range of movement in a joint is limited by the shape of the bones, and this cannot be altered. Within this structural limit, flexibility may be further reduced by muscle tone, by the length of ligaments and by their elasticity. Ligaments are bands of fibrous tissue containing elastic fibres, the latter providing a measure of resilience. Ligaments lie outside of the joint capsule and are attached to the bones, above and below the joint. They are aligned in the direction of the maximum stresses which might be expected at that particular joint.

Ligaments can be torn, and when this happens, previously elastic fibres are replaced by inelastic fibrous tissue. This then gradually shortens so flexibility is reduced. To prevent this from happening, all stretching exercises must be performed slowly. An over-stretched ligament hurts, so no further pressure must be applied. Stretching exercises must always stop short of the point at which actual discomfort is felt. Stretch is applied slowly, and then held at the maximum position for 10 seconds. This can be repeated several times.

By this means, ligaments are stretched in a way that does not damage them. Also the muscle stretch receptors learn how much movement can be allowed, so the protective function of the muscle is not lost.

A good warm-up session must include gentle stretching exercises. Tissues are more flexible following light exercise, and it is always necessary to re-teach ligaments and muscles their limits.

Chapter 6
SOME INDIVIDUAL JOINTS

THE SHOULDER JOINT

This is a rather weak joint. The head of the humerus is rather flat and the socket into which it fits is shallow. The ligaments which locate it are not very strong; in fact they have to be loose in order to accomodate the shoulder's great range of movement. The range of movement is almost entirely limited by bone shape.

The normal range of movement in the shoulder joint is:
- sideways 90° out and 10° in
- backwards about 45°
- forwards 180°
- rotation outwards about 60°
- rotation inwards about 100°

All other movement consists of the arm and shoulderblade moving together and rotating about the *Sterno-clavicular* joint (*Fig. 21*).

The only major injury suffered by the shoulder joint is disloca-

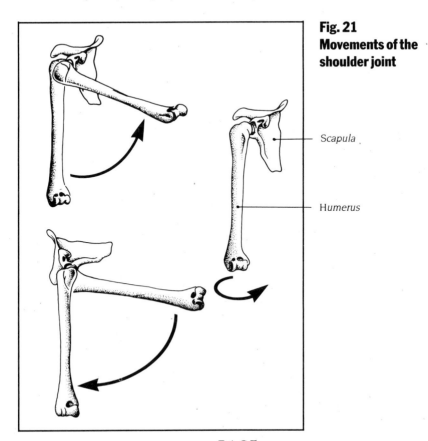

Fig. 21
Movements of the shoulder joint

Scapula

Humerus

tion, the head of the humerus typically moving forwards. This happens when the arm is held out sideways and then pulled back strongly, levering the head of the humerus forwards through the joint capsule and enclosing muscles. The head of the bone eventually comes to lie below the end of the collar bone.

Once the dislocation has been reduced, the joint capsule heals but remains weak. The damaged muscles often do not heal, so subsequent dislocations tend to recur. The shoulder gets weaker each time it dislocates, so less and less force is required. When this eventually becomes too much of a disability, a surgical operation is effective in rebuilding the damaged muscles in front of the joint.

The shoulder is rested in a sling for a day or two but as soon as possible, rehabilitation should begin. The joint must be moved within the limits of discomfort, since this will keep the muscles strong and the ligaments flexible. Training can re-start after three weeks, but no strain should be put on the shoulder until a full pain-free range of movement is possible.

Interestingly, pain from a joint can be felt above the line of that joint. The reason for this will be explained later, but what it means is that pain felt on top of the shoulder is not caused by injury to the shoulder joint. It is more likely to be a spinal injury.

A 'Frozen shoulder' is caused by inflammation of the joint capsule. It tends to occur in martial artists over the age of 40. The shoulder becomes painful and joint movements are more and more restricted until the shoulder is virtually 'frozen'. After a while, movement becomes freer and eventually a full recovery takes place. The whole course of the disease takes about 18 months. Early treatment frequently shortens this period, so the earlier it is recognised and treated, the sooner it recovers.

Symptoms from arthritis of the shoulder usually appear after a prolonged period of immobility caused by a plaster cast. It is therefore very important that shoulder movement is begun as soon and as fully as possible.

THE ELBOW JOINT

The elbow is a very strong joint and in adults, it is very rarely dislocated. In fact, the bones above and below it are more likely to fracture before the joint dislocates.

The elbow joint involves the humerus and the two forearm bones - the *Radius* and the *Ulna*. The main part of the joint is formed by the ulna and the humerus. The ulna head is shaped like a comma, which locates in a hollow at the back of the humerus. The joint is completely lined with cartilage and movement is restricted only by the shape of the bones.

The head of the radius is round, so it can rotate on the side of the ulna. This allows the forearm to turn over (*Fig. 22*).

The commonest injury to the elbow is caused by full power punches made without resistance. If these are uncontrolled, then the punch is stopped by the head of the ulna banging into the hollow at the back of the humerus. This damages the cartilage lining the joint and eventually causes it to break up. Loose pieces of cartilage then float around in the joint, giving rise to pain and loss of elbow extension. Unfortunately, once this process has

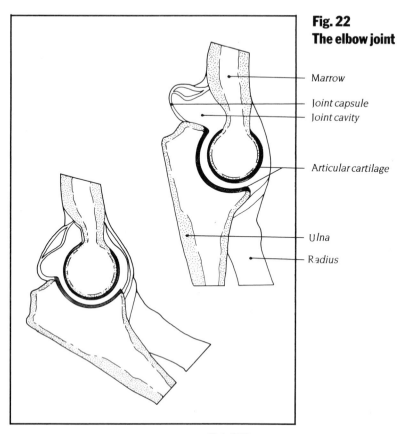

**Fig. 22
The elbow joint**

Marrow

Joint capsule
Joint cavity

Articular cartilage

Ulna
Radius

started, it cannot be cured. If it causes too much disability, an operation to clean out the joint sometimes improves matters.

Many experienced martial artists suffer from this injury. They cannot punch without pain unless they actually hit someone or something.

It is for this reason that punching techniques should be initially taught at slow speed only. Power can be developed by using punching bags and impact pads. However, once control has been developed and techniques can be brought to a stop by muscle power, then full power 'unloaded' techniques can be safely practised.

Sometimes the elbow joint is damaged when the martial artist falls onto a fully extended wrist. This may break the head of the radius. Fortunately it is a relatively trivial injury and if the elbow is kept mobile, the fracture heals quickly and fully.

THE WRIST JOINT

The wrist is a joint between the radius bone of the forearm and a group of eight small bones. These move as one, whilst giving a little spring to the wrist. The wrist is a plain joint, allowing 90° of extension (backwards) and flexion (forwards). With the palm facing forwards, there is about 45° of movement towards the body and 5 - 10° in the opposite direction.

Wrist dislocations are uncommon, and fractures of the radius tend to occur instead. Very rarely, a forcible extension of the wrist causes one of the small bones to dislocate. Sometimes another small bone is broken by a fall onto the extended arm. This fracture cannot be seen on X-ray at the time of injury, though it does appear three weeks or so later when damaged bone has been absorbed. If this injury is not adequately treated, the bone does not heal properly and the hand and wrist are both weakened. Restorative surgery at that stage is not always successful in putting matters right. It is therefore important to re-investigate any wrist injury which is not better after three weeks, even though X-rays at the time of injury were normal.

The ligaments which hold the wrist together do not sprain, but the one on the ulna side becomes inflamed by over-enthusiastic knife-hand practice. This condition is very persistent.

THE HAND

The hand is a fragile structure. Nevertheless, considerable force can be applied to or by the fingers, providing always that the force is applied to the end of a bone, and in a direct line with it. If the bone is even slightly off-line to the force, the fingers are easily dislocated or broken.

A dislocated finger is rather obvious and extremely painful. It is therefore a kindness to reduce the dislocation as soon as possible. This is easily done by pulling hard on the dislocated part in the direction it is pointing, and then bending it straight. If the finger been fractured just below the joint, it may look exactly the same as a dislocation. Even so, your attempt to reduce it will cause no harm provided that the pull is in the right direction. In fact the only damage which is likely to occur may be the black eye you get when the finger's owner objects.

Finger joints can be sprained. If this is ignored, as often happens, a chronic sprain can ensue. The joint so affected will be painful, swollen, and have poor flexion. This condition is very difficult to treat but it can avoided if the initial and simple sprain is given two to three weeks to heal.

A chronic sprain of the thumb is common in martial artists. It occurs most often in the striking-based systems and is caused by repeated minor sprains. These occur when the thumb is not properly tucked away when punching, such as happens when using mitts with thumb-piece. A chronically sprained thumb does not flex properly and is always susceptible to further damage. As with the finger joints, it is much simpler and in the long run, quicker, to treat the initial sprain with the respect it deserves.

The joint at the base of the thumb can be the site of a fracture-dislocation. This injury is caused by a blow on the end of a straight thumb breaking a piece out of the base of the bone and scoring the articular surface. It is unlikely that full range of movement will be restored after this injury.

THE HIP JOINT

The hip is a very strong ball and socket joint (*Fig. 23*). In fact it is so strong that it would be almost impossible within the framework of the martial arts, to apply sufficient force to dislocate it. Movement of the hip is ultimately limited by the shape of the bones. In practice however, the strong muscles and ligaments surrounding it are the usual limiting factors. The hip joint probably benefits the most from gentle stretching exercises. Conversely, the hip can easily be damaged by over-enthusiastic stretching. When its ligaments are torn, it is not uncommon for bone to grow into the resulting scar tissue. This permanently reduces flexibility and it is painful into the bargain.

The major problem which aflicts the hip is arthritis. This causes the articular cartilage to become thin and easily damaged - particularly at the edges. Bone then grows into the site of repair, and onwards into the capsular ligament.

The first symptom of arthritis is pain felt over the joint, usually in the groin though it may be felt lower down the leg. Sometimes the pain is felt over the knee joint. At first this pain is felt only at the

Fig. 23
The hip joint

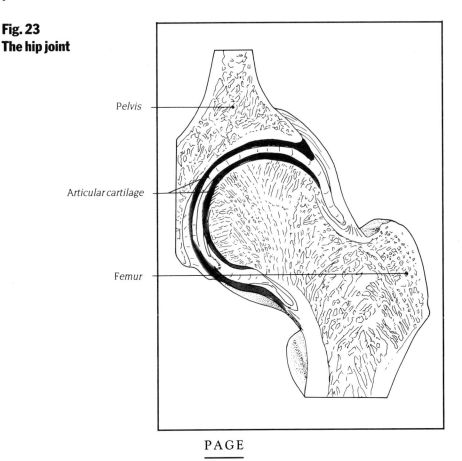

Pelvis

Articular cartilage

Femur

limits of movement but later it becomes constant and is often worse when first moving after rest. First movements to be reduced are hip extension and external rotation. Extension is a backwards movement of the thigh. It is tested with the subject lying flat.

The good leg is flexed against the chest. The last 15° of this movement occurs in the spine such that if the hip extension has been lost, the bad leg lifts up and attempts to push it straight are painful.

External rotation is tested at the same time by pulling the feet up so the thighs are raised to an angle of 45° and the knees are bent. The feet remain resting on the couch. The knees are pushed apart and the distance they move is compared.

Loss of extension is reponsible for causing a limp, and this is reckoned to be the first sign of arthritis of the hip. It is very characteristic and once seen, it will always be recognised again.

Arthritis of the hip is no bar to martial arts practice at any level. In fact, sensible training will benefit the condition. If it is performed within the limits imposed by discomfort, the practice of any technique or exercise will increase the range of pain-free movement in exactly the same way as in a healthy joint.

THE KNEE JOINT

The knee is inherently weak because the shape of the bones do little to prevent them from sliding on each other in any direction. This is aggravated by the fact that the strains imposed upon the knee are very great, arising through force being applied at the end of such long levers as the femur and tibia. For example, pressure on the knee when standing straight is proportional to the body weight. When the knees are bent to a 45° angle, the pressure is proportional to ten times the body weight.

To cope with this, the knee has very strong ligaments which are called:

☐ the *Cruciate* ligaments
☐ the *Collateral* ligaments.

The cruciates are located in the centre of the joint and prevent the tibia from sliding backwards and forwards on the femur. They make the knee work like a huge hinge joint. The collateral ligaments are on each side of the knee and prevent it from bending sideways. Additionally, powerful *Quadriceps* muscles on the front of the thighs end in broad tendons which cover the front and sides of the knee. These are partially attached to the joint ligaments.

The kneecap, or *Patella*, is located inside the quadriceps tendon at the front of the knee. It is not attached to any other bone but is free to slide up and down over the face of the femur. This gives the effect of a pulley action, reducing wear and tear of the tendon.

The knee joint contains the 'Semilunar cartilages'. These help the knee to cope with the jarring caused by walking, running and jumping. They are only attached to the edge of the upper end of the tibia, and are otherwise loose (*Fig. 24*).

The knee rarely dislocates because of the strength of the ligaments. The femur or the tibia will break first. In younger people, in particular girls, the knee cap sometimes dislocates and moves to the outside of the knee. This happens because the quadriceps are powerful muscles and their tendons change from being parallel to

Fig. 24
The knee joint

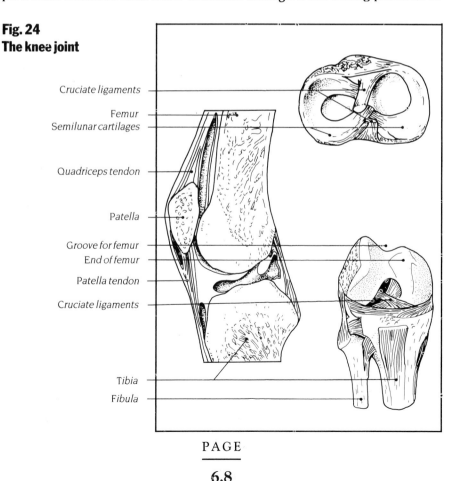

Cruciate ligaments

Femur
Semilunar cartilages

Quadriceps tendon

Patella

Groove for femur
End of femur
Patella tendon
Cruciate ligaments

Tibia
Fibula

the femur to being parallel to the tibia. This angle is greater in women because they have a wider pelvis. When the muscles contract, they pull the kneecap to one side, so a dislocation becomes possible.

In the first instances of mild cases, it may prove possible to improve matters by isometrically strengthening both the quadriceps and the muscles on the inside of the thighs by straight leg lifts to an angle of 15°, with or without a weight on the ankle, and by squeezing a hard ball between the knees. These exercises are able to modify the direction of pull on the kneecap. In more serious cases, a surgical operation may prove necessary.

The main problems which affect the knee stem from damage to the ligaments. Excessive sideways force, or powerful rotation of the knee joint will tear the collateral ligaments, usually at the point where they join onto the bone. This gives rise to pain and tenderness at the site of injury. Recurrent injuries will stretch these ligaments still further until the degree of side-to-side bending of the joint becomes positively alarming.

Rehabilitation consists of maintaining movement within the limits set down by pain, and strengthening the quadriceps muscle. Any possibility of further injury must be avoided until a full range of pain-free movement returns and there is no pain when the ligament is stretched by sideways pressure on the joint.

If a knee injury is accompanied by swelling ('Fluid on the knees'), then damage has been done inside the joint. This could either be to the cruciate ligaments, or to the semi-lunar cartilages. The cruciates may be partially or completely torn by a strong force pushing the tibia backwards or forwards on the femur. This sort of injury could, for example, be caused by a side kick to the front of the straight leg, making contact just below the knee. A complete tear of the cruciates is a serious injury and is best treated by a surgical operation which sews the two parts of the ligament together. This operation involves a prolonged period of immobility, followed by an equally prolonged and laborious period of rehabilitation.

Partial tears of the cruciates can be dealt with in the same way as other sprains of the knee. However, once stretched, the cruciates cannot be compensated for by increasing the tone of the quadriceps. Injury to the cruciates makes the knee unstable and prone to further injury. If this becomes a serious problem, then a surgical operation which grafts in natural or artificial ligaments may produce some improvements.

The cartilage is injured by forcible rotation of the femur on the tibia. This might be caused by the martial artist jumping or turning in the air, then landing and continuing to turn as the foot remains fixed. As a matter of fact, cartilage injuries never occur on their own. If the collateral ligaments are not already torn, the incident which tears the cartilage will tear those too. In minor cases, only the ligament which attaches the cartilage to the tibia, (the *Coronal Ligament*) may become torn, leaving the cartilage in a vulnerable position.

Many cartilage tears will heal themselves if given the chance. This involves resting the joint by doing nothing which causes pain. Rest should continue until a full and pain-free range of movement has been restored. Otherwise, rehabilitation should follow along the same lines as that described above.

The only absolute indication that surgery is needed to remove a cartilage is when there is a history of the joint 'locking'. This happens when a piece of cartilage is trapped between the tibia and femur, and prevents the knee from straightening. When considering surgery, there are two factors to take into account:

☐ when a part or all of the cartilage is removed, it is not replaced by new articular cartilage; the replacement is fibrous, less elastic, and has less shock absorbing qualities.

☐ the operation which removes the cartilage does nothing for the torn ligaments which allowed the cartilage to tear in the first place.

It is my belief that an operation to surgically remove a torn cartilage should be considered only as a last resort, when adequate treatment with rest, mobilisation and exercises have all failed.

Adolescents and young adults, particularly girls, sometimes suffer from a disease in which the cartilage behind the kneecap becomes inflamed and may break up. The only symptom is pain in the knee, first felt by walking downhill, or going downstairs. This gradually gets worse until any activity causes pain. There is no treatment beyond taking pain-killers but fortunately, there is no evidence that this condition leads to arthritis in later life.

THE ANKLE JOINT

The ankle joint is in fact made up of two joints which work at right angles to each other. The upper joint allows the foot to bend up and down, the lower one allows side-to-side movement. In combination, they give a range of movement comparable to that of a ball and socket joint. However they are much stronger because of the shape of the bones (*Fig. 25*). The ankle is held together by strong ligaments both associated with the joint capsule and additionally in the form of strong bands down the sides and in front of the joint. The achilles tendon supports the joint at the back.

The most common ankle injury is a sprain, usually on the outer side of the joint, though it can occur on the inner. Symptoms are swelling and tenderness, with pain on movement. The swelling is

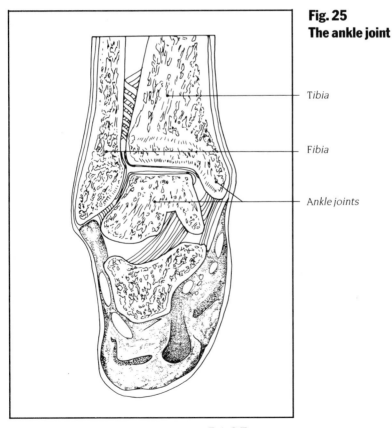

Fig. 25
The ankle joint

Tibia

Fibia

Ankle joints

caused by bleeding from the tear, so extensive bruising is often seen after two to three days. The I.C.E. regime (*see page 4.13*) can help greatly towards rehabilitation by reducing the extent of this bleeding.

In rare cases, the sprain is so severe as to make the ankle joint unstable, thus warranting immobilisation for several weeks in a plaster cast. This makes for a slow recovery. Thankfully such extreme measures are seldom necessary and less drastic cases need not be immobilised in strapping. If at first the sprain is too painful to allow walking, the casualty should simply sit and admire his swollen ankle. He should move it between the pain limits and use ice to reduce both swelling and discomfort.

He should start walking on it as soon as possible, if necessary by only taking short steps. However, he should not limp since this does not allow the ligaments to move naturally over each other and besides, once aquired, a limp is difficult to lose. The martial artist should try to increase the ankle's range of movement at times when it is not weight-bearing and after three weeks, it should be possible to start serious work aimed at restoring the ankle's full range of movement.

A weak ankle is a common after-effect of sprain. The story is typical in that after the sprain has healed, the ankle appears normal though it may have a slightly reduced range of movement. However, a slight strain on the ligaments, such as that which happens when crossing rough ground, causes the ankle to give way. This ankle is actually not weak at all. What happens is that during the healing process, two bands of ligaments have stuck together. When the ankle moves in such a way as to cause a drag on these adhesions, some pain occurs. This causes the leg muscles to relax in a reflex action which tries to prevent further damage being caused to the ligaments. A 'weak' ankle can often be treated by injections, with or without manipulation; the object being to pull the adhesions apart.

THE FOOT

The foot is in many ways like the hand. However, the bones of the foot are much stronger since they must support the weight of the body. The foot is made up of a group of seven small bones which are joined onto five long ones and these in turn, join onto the toes.

The foot has 'Arches' to protect the bones and joints. These give a spring to the foot and absorb a lot of the forces applied. There are in fact, three arches. These run from:

☐ the heel to the base of the big toe

☐ the base of the big toe to the base of the little toe

☐ the base of the little toe back to the heel.

They are formed by the shape of the bones and are maintained by strong ligaments and muscles in the sole of the foot. When standing, body weight is taken by:

☐ the heel

☐ the outer edge of the foot

☐ the ball of the foot.

This is easily seen in the print of a wet foot on a smooth, hard floor.

The arches are concerned with the mechanics of walking and running, both of which actions are not quite as straightforward as you may think. The sequence of events which take place during one step are:

☐ the heel strikes the floor first, and takes all the body weight

☐ the weight is taken on the outer edge of the foot and transfered to the outer side of the ball of the foot; at this time the foot is pointing straight ahead, or turned slightly inwards

☐ the weight then transfers across the ball of the foot to the inner edge, at the base of the big toe; during this transfer, the foot turns slightly inwards

☐ the big toe transmits the power for the next step.

This sequence is most important in protecting the bones, ligaments and joints of the foot from strain. Failure in its operation is a common cause of foot pain during running. The soles of the shoes will show if there is any fault and there should be no excessive wear on either side of the sole or heel. If wear is discovered, then the condition which causes it can be corrected by building up the relevant parts so the foot is made to turn correctly. Building up the heel will ensure it strikes the ground first. Building up the inner/outer edges of the sole will make the sole of the foot turn inwards/outwards respectively.

When the arches are deficient or missing, the outcome is 'Flat feet'. This comes about as a result of the ligaments being stretched and the muscles in the sole of the foot weakening. The foot aches more and more during standing and walking, but when it becomes completely flat and the arches are lost, the ligaments are no longer under strain under strain and the foot becomes pain-free. At this stage, body weight is taken over the whole area of the sole and normal mechanism of walking is lost. This leads to an ungainly gait and a reduced mobility during walking and running. Additionally the foot's shock-absorbing system is lost, so the likelihood of damage to the bones, joints and soft tissue is increased. This in turn causes pain and activity is severely limited.

A flat foot cannot be diagnosed purely by the appearance of the foot. In some cases the foot appears completely flat, yet the arch is clearly seen when the subect stands on tip-toe. This works as for a normal foot and can be ignored if it is symptom-free.

As I have previously mentioned, the foot aches when the ligaments are actually stretching, and there is tenderness where they attach to the ball of the foot and under the heel. By strengthening these muscles, some of the strain can be relieved so pain is eased. Suitable exercises for this might be:
□ walking about in bare feet for ten to fifteen minutes on tip-toe
□ picking up objects such as matchboxes with the toes
□ drawing and writing with a pencil grasped between the toes.
These exercises must be repeated several times a day. If symptoms persist, pain can be eased by putting an arch support into the shoes. Having said that, do realise that this takes all the loading from the muscles, so that they weaken and the foot becomes flat more rapidly.

Over 45 years of age, fibrous shock-absorbing pads under the heel bone and ball of the foot begin to wear thin. This tends to happen more under the heel. Normal activity may then cause bruising and inflammation where ligaments attach to the bones, so walking becomes difficult and in some cases, impossible. Treatment consists of giving injections directly into the inflamed ligaments, and wearing foam padding under the heel and ball of the foot. When symptoms first appear, a period of rest followed by the use of foam pads may prevent the condition from getting worse. I doubt whether anyone suffering from this complaint could train in bare feet.

Two kinds of foot deformity can be present at birth. The first is when the feet do not point the right way. Most commonly, the foot points downwards and inwards. Some tendons are too short, others too long, so the foot cannot be pushed into a normal position. The reason this happens is not known but it can be corrected by using splints and by surgically lengthening or shortening the tendons where appropriate.

The second type of foot deformity occurs when the arches of the foot become greatly exaggerated, often to the degree that only the heel and the ball of the foot are in contact with the ground. This condition is caused by paralysis of certain muscles in the foot and leg and is a common feature of mild *spina bifida*. Unfortunately, no treatment is possible.

Neither deformity is a bar to martial arts training, though some techniques and exercises may have to be modified.

Toe deformity can be acquired in later life. Most commonly the toes become bent towards the outer edge of the foot as a result of wearing shoes which are not wide enough. When toes are pushed sideways, they pull on those tendons which flex and to extend them will actually increase the deformity. After a while, the ends of the bones forming the joints alter their shape to conform to the direction in which the toe is pointing. The deformity is then fixed and can only be corrected by surgical operation. Again, these are no bar to training, though exercises and techniques may have to be modified.

Corns are overgrowths of skin resulting from pressure inflicted by badly-fitting shoes. Prevention is better than cure.

Many fractures of the foot have already been mentioned and apart from these, injuries to the foot follow the same pattern as those to the hand. Direct violence can both fracture and dislocate bones in the foot. Probably most common are sprains of the toes. These are frequently chronic, though the results are even more disabling. During walking and running, all the stepping-off force is applied through the ball of the big toe. To accomplish this, the toe must extend for at least 45°, and preferably more. When this is not possible, weight is taken on the toe itself and strong leverage is applied to the sprained joint. To compensate, the foot turns outwards and by this means, the strength of the 'push-off' is lessened.

If the big toe is sprained, the following exercise may be of some value in restoring a full range of movement:

☐ pull the toe hard out of the foot and in a straight line
☐ whilst still pulling, bend the toe up and down through 10-15° for 60 seconds; this stimulates the production of lubricating fluid in the joint
☐ then gently bend the toe to its flexibility limits.

Repeat this exercise five times and repeat the whole sequence four to five times each day until the toe is fully mobile once more.

THE SPINE

The spine is a chain of thirty-two bones (*Vertebrae*) which can be divided into five groups:

☐ cervical (neck) 7 bones
☐ dorsal (chest) 12 bones
☐ lumbar 5 bones
☐ sacral 5 bones
☐ coccygeal 3 bones

Fig. 26
Three views of a lumbar vertebra

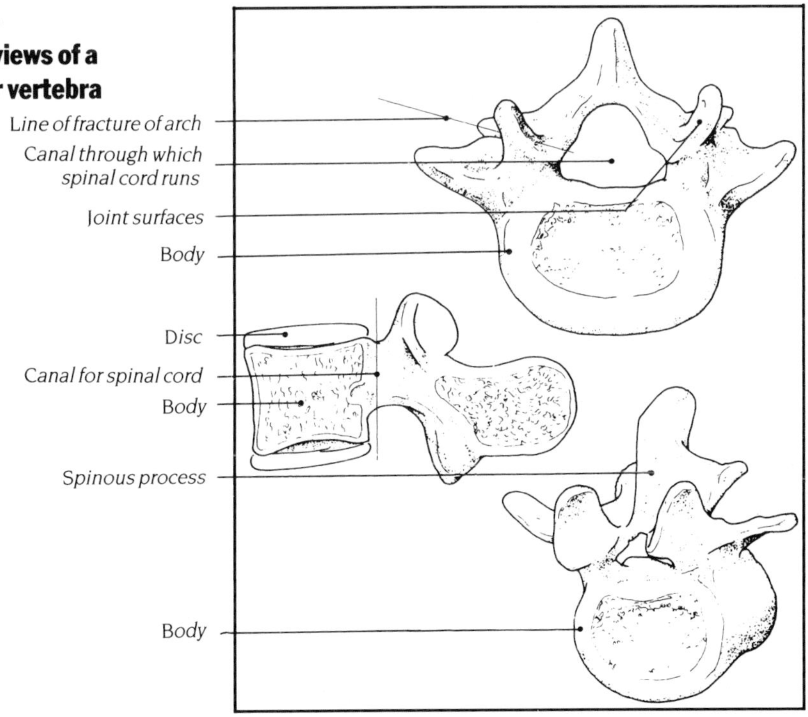

Line of fracture of arch
Canal through which spinal cord runs
Joint surfaces
Body
Disc
Canal for spinal cord
Body
Spinous process
Body

The coccygeal bones are fused together to form the *Coccyx*. This is all that remains of a tail. The sacral bones are fused to form the *Sacrum* and this is where the legs connect with the trunk, via the pelvis and sacro-iliac joints. All the body's weight is transmitted through it. The other vertebrae remain as individual bones and all have certain characteristics in common.

The parts of a vertebra are:
☐　the body
☐　the neural arch
☐　two transverse processes
☐　the spinous process (*Fig. 26*).

The vertebral body is a disc of bone above and below which are the *Intervertebral discs*. Body weight is transmitted through it. The neural arch is attached to the back of the vertebral body and forms the back of the channel through which the spinal cord passes. Above and below and on both sides are the joint faces. These articulate with the vertebrae immediately above and below. The transverse processes are situated on either side and at the same level as the neural arch is attached to the vertebral body. These form attachments for the powerful spinal muscles. The spinous process projects out from the back of the neural arch. It is attached to the spinal muscles. The spinous processes can be felt as knobs along the length of the spine.

The vertebrae become smaller as they ascend from the sacrum to the neck because the weight which each supports grows gradually less. Each part of the spine has a separate function. The lumbar spine forms a strong anchor for the spinal, hip and leg muscles. It is capable of a wide range of movement in the forwards direction ('Flexion'), backwards direction ('Extension') and sideways movement ('Side flexion'). The dorsal spine provides anchorage for the ribs. Because these have a splinting effect, movement in this section is confined to rotation. In fact, nearly all of the spine's rotation occurs in this region. The cervical spine supports most of the weight of the shoulders and arms. It is the most mobile region of the spine, and has good mobility in all places.

The cervical/dorsal and the lumbar/sacral junctions bring together mobile and less mobile regions. For this reason, they are frequent sites of injury.

SOME INDIVIDUAL JOINTS

Seen from the front, the spine appears straight. From the side, however, it is a series of curves (*Fig. 27*). The following joints are located directly above and below each other:
☐ the joint between the skull and the spine
☐ the joint between the cervical and dorsal spine
☐ the joint between the dorsal and lumbar spine
☐ the joint between the lumbar and sacral spine
☐ the hip joint
☐ the heel

Fig. 27
The spine and
good posture

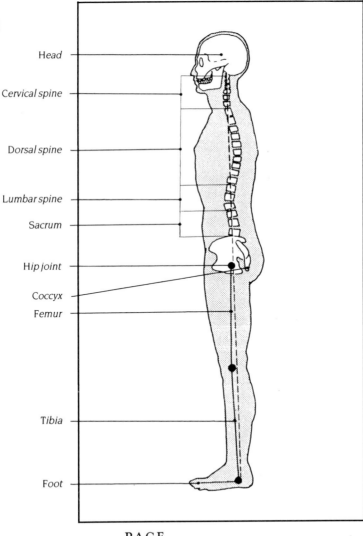

The vertebrae are so shaped that this is the position of rest for the spine, and only a minimum of muscle action is needed to maintain it. This is the situation that exists when posture is good. In any other position, the back is unstable and requires muscular effort to maintain it.

The rims of adjacent vertebral bodies are joined by a strong ligament which forms a sealed compartment filled with thick, gelatinous material. This is called the *Intervertebral disc*. It acts both as a shock absorber and it allows one vertebra to move on another. The material in the discs gets harder with increasing age, so some flexibility is lost and shocks are transmitted more readily through the spine. This loads extra strain on the other joints.

A prolapsed disc occurs when the ligaments holding it in place weaken. This allows the disc material to bulge out at the back of the disc. The bulge can press on the spinal cord, or on a spinal nerve, depending upon where it occurs. This pressure causes pain in the area where the nerve has come from, and weakness in the muscles to which it is going. It is known as *Sciatica*. Note that this pain is not felt in the back, but rather it occurs in the leg, thigh and occasionally in the buttock. Scatica nearly always requires surgical treatment but the younger person may be able to avoid this by resting for three weeks flat on his back.

Lumbago is a Latin word meaning simply 'a pain in the back'. The condition is now generally referred to simply as 'L.B.P.' (Lower back pain). A discussion as to the causes, treatment and management of L.B.P. would take a book all by itself. In fact, many dozens of books have been written on the subject. Suffice it to say that most of the pain comes from muscle spasm and any treatment which relieves that spasm, be it drugs, massage, manipulation, acupuncture, is the correct treatment. The most important thing is to prevent a recurrence, so begin by trying to recall what may have brought on the attack, and avoid doing that in the future.

Start gentle movements of the back in all directions as soon as possible, going gently to the point of discomfort. Strenuous stretching exercises should be avoided until a good range of movement has been restored. Later, the muscles of the back can be strengthened in the following manner:

☐ the subject lies face downwards and lifts the head and

shoulders as far off the floor as possible (exercises the muscles of the upper back)
☐ from the same position, the straight legs are lifted (exercises the lower back)
☐ from the same position, both shoulders and legs are lifted together
☐ each position must be held for five seconds, and repeated five to ten times with a short rest between.

In cases where the tissues causing the muscle spasm are inflamed, pain can often be felt down the thigh and leg. This however, is not sciatica because the nerves are not involved. The only useful treatment for this condition is steroid injections into the tissues.

Fractures of the spine are not common. Crush fractures of the vertebral body usually result from direct violence, such as by falling onto the feet with the legs held rigid. The vertebrae most usually affected by this sort of accident are in the dorsal or upper lumbar spine. Crush fractures are painful and require several weeks rest. The vertebrae affected frequently collapse and end up wedge-shaped. Despite this, little disability occurs.

Fractures of the transverse process in the lumbar region occur as a result of muscular action. In fact, an intense spasm can pull a transverse process away from the vertebral body. This is very painful and requires prolonged immobility for it to heal. The back may be weak afterwards.

Fractures across the neural arch occur in the lumbar, dorsal and cervical regions. The fracture line passes between the joints of the upper and lower surfaces of the vertebra. If both sides are broken, the spine becomes unstable and the region above the fracture can slip forwards. Movement of the spine is restricted and painful. This frequently requires an operation to fuse that part of the spine.

When this type of fracture occurs in the cervical spine, the outcome can be more serious. If the top part of the spine slides forwards, it will cut across the spinal canal and sever the spinal cord. This will cause a complete and permanent paralysis, plus loss of all sensation below the level of the fracture. It may be that this does not happen at the time the injury has been sustained. If this is the case, then keeping the neck extended (bending it a little backwards) will keep the fracture stable and damage to the spinal cord will not occur.

Frequently, a casualty suffering from this injury will be unconscious. If he is not, then he will complain of severe pain at the site of the injury and possibly of tingling or numbness of the hands and feet. It is most important that he should not be moved without expert assistance if a fracture of the neck is suspected.

In the lumbar region, such fractures sometimes affect one side only. This is unexpectedly found in L.B.P. sufferers, and most in people with a high degree of mobility in the spine. There is no treatment beyond taking pain-killers and there are no long-term effects beyond a slight weakness in the spine.

THE PELVIC JOINTS

The only joints of consequence in the pelvis are the two *Sacro-iliacs* which are situated one on each side of the base of the spine (the *Sacrum*). The joints face sideways and are right-angle shaped, with joint surfaces which are undulating rather than straight. This allows the pelvis to tilt backwards and forwards through an angle of about 15°. Strong ligaments firmly hold the joint and prevent it from moving too far. Many people think that this joint is of little importance, and that this fixation does not matter. I believe very strongly that this joint has a very important part to play in the overall flexibility of the lower spine and the hips.

The sacro-iliac may be over-rotated during certain martial art techniques such as the high roundhouse kick. When correctly executed, this kick uses a perfectly safe sideways-lift of the thigh (*Adduction*). Should, however, the supporting foot not rotate sufficiently, the pelvis cannot move with the kick and a strong turning force is applied to the sacro-iliacs. Things get even worse if the martial artist tries to keep his body upright during the kick. In my opinion, many so-called 'Hamstring injuries' are in fact caused by immobility of the sacro-iliac joint.

Chapter 7
THE NERVOUS SYSTEM

THE NERVOUS SYSTEM

The nervous system (*Fig. 28*) is composed of three parts:
☐ the brain
☐ the spinal cord
☐ the nerves

Like all the tissues of the body, the nervous system consists of billions of cells. Each cell is made up of a body and a number of fibres which join one nerve cell to another. This allows nervous impulses to be sent on. The join is not a physical one; rather it is a chemical one and is called a *Synapse*. When the nerve impulse arrives at the end of a fibre, it causes a chemical reaction, and it is this which stimulates the other nerve cells. The reaction is helped by enzymes and takes place very quickly.

All nerve cell bodies are located in the 'Central Nervous System' ('C.N.S.'). This is the name given to the brain and spinal cord. When these are cut open, they are seen to contain two types of tissue called 'Grey matter' and 'White matter'. Grey matter consists of

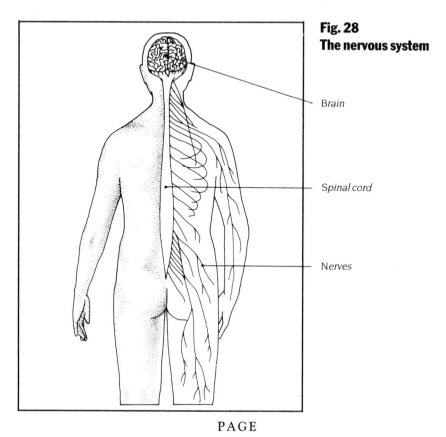

Fig. 28
The nervous system

Brain

Spinal cord

Nerves

nerve cells only and white matter is made from bundles of nerve fibres. The 'nerves' which run through the body and limbs are in fact, bundles of fibres only.

A nerve cell (*Fig. 29*) can be one of two types, sensory, or motor. Motor cells have one main fibre and when they are stimulated, an impulse travels down the fibre to a nerve ending on muscle cells. This causes them to contract. Sensory cells also have a main fibre which in this case ends in a sensory organ of some sort. These sensory cells have many smaller fibres which connect them with neighbouring cells. In this way, a nerve impulse can be passed to different parts of the brain and spinal cord, and also to motor cells.

The spinal cord is the communication channel between the brain and the rest of the body. The nerve cells are all found in an 'H' shaped core running up the centre of the cord. They are surrounded by bundles of large fibres taking information to and from the brain. All information coming into the body and all instructions

Fig. 29
Nerve cell

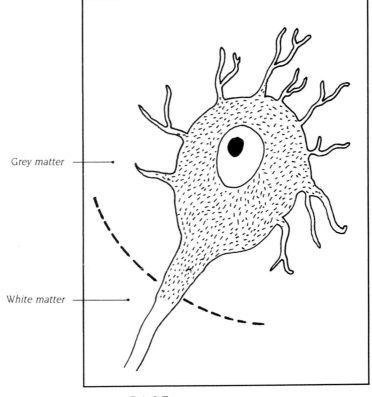

Grey matter

White matter

given by the brain pass through this distribution centre.

For some peculiar reason, the nerve fibres cross from one side of the body to the other as they journey from peripheral nerve to brain, and vice versa. Some sensory pathways cross over immediately on entering the spinal cord, others, such as the motor pathways, do so in the brain itself. Thus, when you burn the fingers of your right hand, the left side of the brain records the fact.

THE BRAIN

The brain can be divided into four parts. These are:

☐ the fore-brain
☐ the mid-brain
☐ the hind-brain
☐ the *Cerebellum*.

The fore-brain is the largest part. It consists of 2 halves which are known as the *Cerebral hemispheres*. Together, they form the *Cerebrum*. The hemispheres are covered with deep fissures which increase the surface area. The grey matter of nerve cells forms a thin skin on the surface of the cerebral hemispheres and because of the increased surface area, there is room for a great many cell bodies in what is called the *Cortex*. Beneath the cortex is the white matter of nerve fibres. The cortex is divided into areas which are

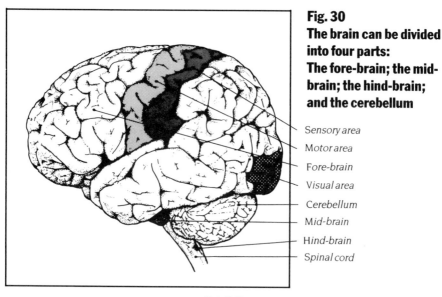

Fig. 30
The brain can be divided into four parts:
The fore-brain; the mid-brain; the hind-brain; and the cerebellum

Sensory area

Motor area

Fore-brain

Visual area

Cerebellum

Mid-brain

Hind-brain

Spinal cord

concerned with memory, decision-making and all voluntary activity. The mid- and hind-brain are extensions of the spinal cord and as such, the white matter is on the outside. The enclosed grey matter is broken up into separate bodies.

The mid-brain is the distribution centre for the brain. It receives signals from all parts of the cerebrum and from the spinal cord. The hind-brain is concerned with functions which operate without conscious thought. To accomplish this, the hind-brain has a number of centres which are responsible for certain activities. There is, for example, a respiratory and a cardiac centre, both of which respond automatically to signals received from the body. The cerebellum coordinates all muscle activity.

The fore-brain, mid-brain and hind-brain have all developed from the most primitive types of brain, such as are found in earthworms. The cerebellum is a much later addition, appearing first in the fish, where it coordinates the muscular action used in swimming (*Fig. 30*).

THE AUTONOMIC NERVOUS SYSTEM

This system has its own network of of nerve cells and fibres. All the internal organs of the body are supplied with sensory nerve endings and these allow the system to monitor such things as blood pressure, heart rate and all the other variables in the body's internal environment. The system connects with the mid-brain from where it receives emotional stimuli. It is this connection which, for example, makes the face flush and then go pale under the influence of extreme anger. This gives a clue to the overall function of the autonomic nervous system which can be summarised as readying the body to cope with the outside environment.

The autonomic nervous system is made of 2 parts:

□ the *Sympathetic*

□ the *Parasympathetic*

These work in opposite directions. The sympathetic system prepares the body for fight or flight, the parasympathetic prepares it for rest. The sympathetic system speeds the heart rate up, the parasympathetic slows it down. The effects of the sympathetic can be seen before the physical need is present. Thus the martial artist will have a racing pulse before the grading is about to start. However, once started, his pulse slows according to physical effort. Similarly he may begin sweating, even though there is as yet no excess heat to get rid of.

THE SENSE ORGANS
The eye is the most important of all the sense organs (*Fig. 31*). Functionally, the eye can be said to consist of 4 important parts. These are:
☐ the Cornea
☐ the Iris
☐ the Lens
☐ the Retina.
The cornea is simply a clear window in the eye, through which light

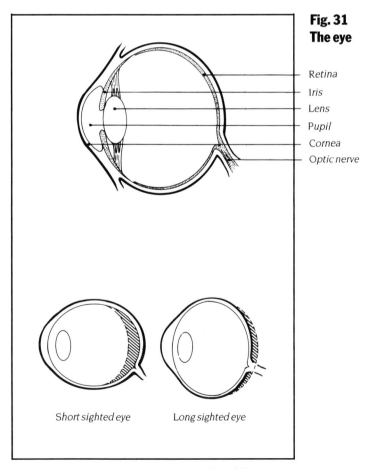

Fig. 31
The eye

Retina
Iris
Lens
Pupil
Cornea
Optic nerve

Short sighted eye   Long sighted eye

can pass. It is easily damaged and like all tissues, it heals by forming fibrous scar tissue. This is opaque, so extensive scarring of the cornea results in defective sight. The iris is the round, coloured tissue lying on the lens. The black hole in the centre - the Pupil - is widened or narrowed by the action of muscles in the iris. The iris has two functions:

☐ to adjust the amount of light entering the eye so as to get the best vision without damage to the retina

☐ when looking at close objects, to concentrate the light on the centre of the lens and give a sharper focus.

The lens focusses light onto the retina. Its curvature is altered by muscles and when they contract, the lens is pulled thinner, so light from objects farther away is focussed. When the muscles relax, the elasticity of the lens pulls it into a fatter shape, so that nearby objects come into focus. The normal range of sharp vision is between 10 inches and infinity. However, the lens becomes more rigid with age, so when the muscles relax, it does not curve sufficiently. As a result, near focus is lost and the closest distance for sharp vision may extend to 24 inches or more. Many people over 45 years of age are obliged to either wear glasses for reading, or to hold their newspaper at arms' length. Later on, the muscles are unable to pull the lens thin enough, so distance vision is affected and driving glasses are required.

The retina is the sensory part of the eye. This consists of a layer of nerve endings which are sensitive to light. Near the centre of the retina is an area of 1 - 2 millimetres in diameter, where vision is sharpest. Elsewhere in the retina it is not so acute. To test this, fix your eyes on some object on the other side of the room. Notice what objects appear at the edge of your field of vision. You will discover that they are not easily recognisable until you actually turn your head to look directly at them. As a matter of fact, at the edges of vision, a movement can be easily seen, though what is moving may not be recognised. Notice how narrow is the angle in which vision is sharp.

Messages from the retina pass along nerve fibres which collect together into the *Optic nerve*. This carries the message to a collection of nerve cells in the mid-brain from where they are distributed. The main part which receives impulses from the retina is called the *Visual cortex* at the back of the cerebrum (*see Fig. 30*). This is where the image first reaches the conscious level. The connections are so arranged that the left side of the brain sees what the right eye sees, and vice versa (*Fig. 32*).

Long sight and short sight occur as a result of the eyeball not being spherical. Long sight occurs when the eyeball is flattened in a front-to-back direction. In this case, a nearby image is focussed behind the retina, rather than on it. Distance vision is unaffected. Short sight is the reverse of this. The eyeball is stretched from front to back, so far objects are focussed in front of the retina (*Fig. 31*).

The skin is full of nerve endings which function as sense receptors. There are several different varieties, so the brain is able to distinguish between a light touch and a heavy touch, between heat and hold etc. The receptors are very sensitive and and need only a slight stimulus to send messages. Pain receptors are much

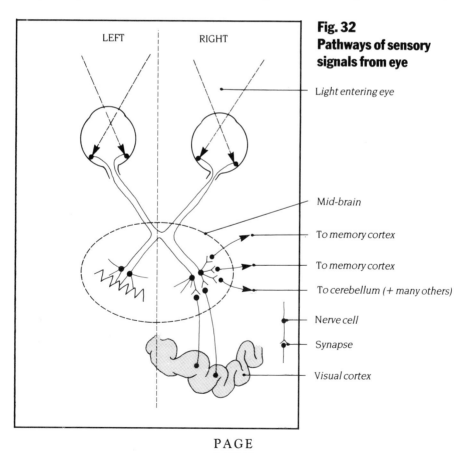

Fig. 32
Pathways of sensory signals from eye

LEFT   RIGHT

Light entering eye

Mid-brain

To memory cortex

To memory cortex

To cerebellum (+ many others)

Nerve cell

Synapse

Visual cortex

smaller and require greater stimulation.

Whatever the sensation, the signal passes along the fibre to the nerve cell, which is situated close to the spinal cord. From there, it goes via another fibre to a special area of the mid-brain. It is then further distributed to the *Sensory cortex*, the motor areas and the memory areas. The sensory cortex is that part of the brain which visualises the the site of the sensation (*Fig. 33*). Areas of the body which have more critical sensation (the lips and the fingers) occupy a disproportionately large area of the cortex.

The feeling of pain is not recognised in the cortex but is 'appreciated' (if that is the right word) in the mid-brain itself. People with a disease affecting the mid-brain feel all sensations other than pain. It seems as though the cortex acts simply to localise a sensation. Any message containing emotional content, such as pain or pleasure, is processed in the mid-brain centre.

Fig. 33
Sensory pathways in brain

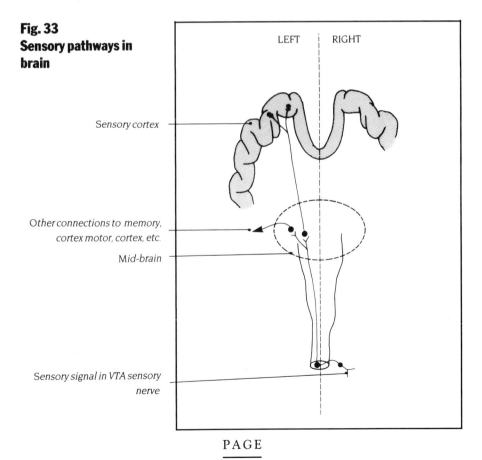

Sensory cortex

Other connections to memory, cortex motor, cortex, etc.

Mid-brain

Sensory signal in VTA sensory nerve

LEFT   RIGHT

Pain is different from any other touch sensation because if you feel a pinprick for example, it is possible to see what is producing it. On the other hand, if someone tells me that he has a pain in his back, there is no way that I can tell him he hasn't!

Pain is useful because it protects the body. It arises from a stimulation of sufficient strength potentially to cause damage to the body. Unfortunately, the cortex can only visualise the skin areas, so that pain arising from a deeper structure is localised to a corresponding skin area.

Confusion arises because man is basically constructed in segments, in some ways like an earthworm. We look different because our segments have become stretched and twisted to produce arms, legs, a nose, and any other structures projecting from what is basically a purely tubular shape. Pain is localised in the same 'segment' as that in which it originates. This is simple in the case of a sprained ankle; the pain is felt in the skin over the joint. It is less simple in the case of a ruptured spleen where the pain is felt in the shoulder; or in the case of a damaged lumbar spinal joint, in the foot!

Anyone can have too much of a good thing. Once a pain has registered potential damage and the stimulus is removed, the pain is no longer useful. It is, to put it mildly, an inconvenience. The body has its own mechanisms for suppressing pain. The brain can produce chemicals called *Endorphins* from a part of the mid-brain, and these anaesthetise the the injured part. Drugs such as morphia do exactly the same thing. The brain can also send signals which effectively block the painful sensations at the nerve which is originating them. If the brain is otherwise occupied, a pain can be 'forgotten'.

Pain-relieving mechanisms are under the brain's control. This is demonstrated by the fact that pain can be abolished by hypnosis. Hypnosis is a state where the mind is very susceptible to suggestion. Tell a hypnotised person that he feels no pain, and it goes away. This abolition can persist even when the person is no longer hypnotised.

Pain suppression is also something that can be trained in and many martial artists achieve this by constantly thumping each other. It certainly does work. However, whether this is a good thing, and whether the benefits outweigh the physical damage is something I will leave to you to decide.

VOLUNTARY MOVEMENTS

Voluntary movements are those which the individual wishes to make. They start from a part of the cerebral cortex known as the 'Motor cortex' (*Fig. 34*). This is organised in such a way that it originates whole movements, rather than contractions of individual muscles. Each part of the motor cortex deals with a specific part of the body. Imagine the body drawn on the motor cortex, with the head at the bottom, and the feet disappearing down the divide between the 2 halves of the brain. The individual thus drawn would be a most peculiar shape! This is because the area devoted to the part of the body depends upon the intricacy of movement in that part, not its actual size. Therefore the mouth,

Fig. 34
Motor pathways in brain

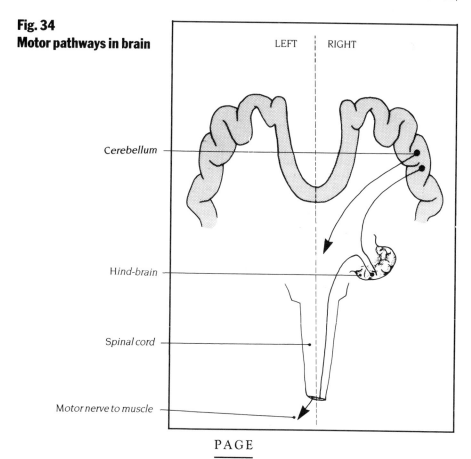

LEFT   RIGHT

Cerebellum

Hind-brain

Spinal cord

Motor nerve to muscle

tongue and face (including the muscles involved in speaking), take up as much space on the cortex as the arms, and far more than the trunk and legs.

The signal travels from the cortex to the cerebellum. It is difficult to over-estimate the importance of the cerebellum in the whole process of voluntary movement. Imagine the manager of a large company issuing a single order that involved many departments in producing a single result. All the sub-managers would rush around to do their bit and the result would most likely be total confusion! In the comparable situation of the body, the cerebellum co-ordinates all movement, so that signals are sent to the right muscles, at the right strength and in the right sequence, so the required movement is performed smoothly. Nerve impulses from the cerebellum pass down the spinal cord to the motor nerves, until they reach the muscles concerned with the action (*see Fig. 34*).

Diseases of the cerebellum result in movements which are slow, hesitant, jerky and often finish in the wrong place. This unfortunate situation is known as *Ataxia*. Automatic movements, on the other hand, may still be performed perfectly.

Many movements are semi-voluntary. This means that they can be started automatically, or voluntarily. The movements produced may not be appreciated at a conscious level, though they could be. Most of us will at some time, have found ourselves in a particular position without having any idea of how this came about. This is because in a chain of unconscious operations, the body has sensed the start and finish positions, started the necessary motor sequences, and maintained balance throughout. It may only be when someone remarks on it that the action is noticed at a conscious level.

REFLEXES

Put your finger on a very hot surface and 2 things happen. First you pull your finger away quickly, and then you say "Ouch!", or words to that effect. The order in which these happen is important and means that you pulled your finger away before you realised it was being burned. This happened too quickly for instructions to have been sent by the brain. What is called a 'Spinal reflex' has occurred

(*Fig. 35*) to protect the body.

To take another example, and one which most people are familiar with, you sit with your knees crossed and someone taps the tendon below the kneecap. This causes your foot to kick forwards. This happens because the receptors in the muscle are stretched by the tap and a signal from the stretch sensors travels to the spinal cord and triggers a muscle contraction.

Consider next, a pair of reflexes associated with the eye-blink. In the first, the cornea of the eye is touched with a piece of cotton wool. The eyelid immediately blinks. This is the same as the escape reflex described above. The second reflex occurs when an object moves towards the eyes. Again they blink shut. In this case, the sequence of events is quite different. The image of the approaching object is focussed on the retina and transmitted to the visual centre. There it is passed to the cortex where it comes to the conscious level. At the same time it is sent to the memory areas of the cortex where it is recognised as a possible danger to the eye. A message passes to the motor cortex, telling the eyelid to blink.

Fig. 35
A spinal reflex arc

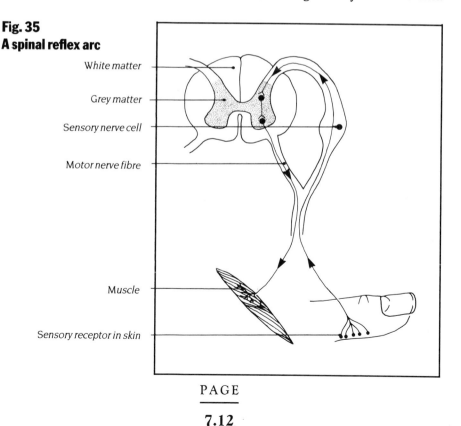

White matter

Grey matter

Sensory nerve cell

Motor nerve fibre

Muscle

Sensory receptor in skin

Both reflexes are similar insofar as the stimulus causes the eyes to blink. The second example involves recognition of the danger to the eye and this is reflected in the time taken. The first reflex took 40 milliseconds (where 1 millisecond is a thousandth of a second). The second took over 6 times longer at 250 milliseconds.

MAINTAINING BALANCE

As I have already mentioned, stretch receptors measure both length and tension in the tendons and muscles. By putting all this information together, the body knows precisely about the posture. Measuring the changes in signals indicates changes in posture. However, the tendon and muscle receptors are too crude and slow to be able to cope with the maintenance of balance when standing on 2 feet. In this case, the majority of information is provided by sensations of pressure on the soles of the feet.

A healthy person can close his eyes and stand upright and steady, with feet together. When sensation in the soles of the feet is lost, as can happen in certain forms of nerve inflammation, the sufferer starts swaying about and can only stop himself from falling by separating his feet or opening his eyes. This is because the eyes act as an organ of balance by taking a visual reference from the environment. Some of you will know how difficult it is to keep your balance in a fairground fun-house where all the angles of wall and floor etc are deliberately distorted.

The ears also contain an organ of balance which keeps the head in an upright position through reflex action. By combining this information with that received from muscle/tendon stretch receptors, the body's posture can be visualised. It may come as a surprise to learn that the ears are the least important of the organs of balance. Even if both are destroyed, the sufferer can still walk, run, or ride a bike with no apparent disability. The only time he may get into difficulties is when he tries to swim. Water reduces the force of gravity and the body does not get the right signals from the stretch receptors.

All translation of the incoming signals and organisation of the muscular response to them takes place in the spinal cord. The only input provided by the brain is to try and recover the balance, once it has been lost. This actually comes from the mid-brain and so is not a conscious activity.

Walking and running are voluntary activities but their execution is automatic, and controlled by the spinal cord. This senses the constantly changing posture and balance, and produces the correct sequence of muscle activity. These activities all have to be learned by a baby. In exactly the same way, the martial artist has to learn how to perform a technique such as the roundhouse kick. The body must feel the patterns of sensation and make the required muscular actions until after sufficient repetitions have been made, the action is imprinted upon the nerve cells. Thereafter, it is only necessary for the brain to send the message "I want to kick Fred in the ear", and the action is as good as done.

Disorders of balance result in *Vertigo*, or dizziness. When the organs of balance disagree and this is brought to the attention of the conscious mind, vertigo follows. The body thinks it is going up and down, or round and round when in fact, it is stationary. Diseases of the ear lead it to send wrong signals to the brain, saying perhaps that the head is tilted to the side, when the eyes and neck tell it that the head is straight. Arthritis may tell the neck that it is tilted to one side, but the eyes and ears say it isn't. In the funhouse mentioned above, the eyes say that the room is tilted but the neck and ears say it is straight. Vertigo results when the conflict between signals is too great. In many cases, the cause cannot be removed and one can only try to suppress the symptoms.

CONSCIOUSNESS, UNCONSCIOUSNESS & SLEEP

This is a subject which no-one knows a great deal about. All that can be said is that in a conscious state, you know what is happening around you because of sensory inputs in terms of sights, sounds, temperature, touch etc. Unconsciousness is a state in which you are unaware of your surroundings. This is confirmed by measuring the brain's electrical activity. When you are conscious, this activity is very high; when you are unconscious it is very low, and when you are dead, it is absent altogether!

It seems that during sleep, the brain's store of nutrients, chemicals and enzymes is replenished, ready for the next day's hard thinking. Sleep is different from unconsciousness and the electrical pattern reveals that although activity is generally at a low pitch, there are several intervals each of a few minutes' duration when activity becomes intense. That is when 'refreshing' of the brain is taking place. Many drugs induce sleep whilst suppressing these active phases. That is why many sleeping pills cause you to wake up tired, slow, and with a hangover.

The total length of time you sleep does not matter. Some people are happy with 2 hours' sleep, others with 12. The only thing of importance is that you wake up refreshed each morning.

MEMORY & LEARNING

Memory is a function of the cerebral cortex only. Like many things to do with the brain, exactly how it works is unknown. Certain areas of the cortex have a specific function, such as the motor cortex, the sensory cortex etc. Provided these are not touched, large areas of the cortex can be removed with no apparent effect on the memory. It has proved impossible to associate any part of the cortex with any particular type of memory - visual, auditory, touch etc. - they all seem to be mixed up.

All incoming signals go through the mid-brain and are passed to various parts of the brain, including the sensory cortex. Some signals appear to be recorded in the cortex from which they can be recalled. These signals are said to be 'Memorised' but how this happens is again, not known. Certainly they are not stored as in a computer, where electrical signals run around in circles until they are tapped. Instead signals may be stored through the action of chemicals and particularly the enzymes, which may transfer signals from cell to cell.

It is known that 2 or more signals may be recorded near together in time and possibly near together on the cortex. When this happens, an association seems to be set up between them, so one recalls the other.

The setting up of such associations is the principle behind all commercial courses aimed at improving the memory, and behind the obscene rhymes which generations of medical students use to help them remember human anatomy.

Consider now the following two facts:

□ repetition of the same signal, or series of signals will imprint itself on the cortex and be memorised

□ setting up associations can assist this process.

Let us follow this a little further and relate it to skill training in the martial arts.

A fist approaches your face. The sensory signal is distributed to the various parts of the brain.....and the fist hits you on the nose! This produces more input to the sensory cortex which inteprets it as a pain in the nose. It goes also to the memory areas where the following association is made:

□ a fist approaching means a pain in the nose.

When this happens again, the image is recognised, the association is made and a message is sent to the motor cortex. This sends a message to the cerebellum to duck, or to put your hands over your nose. Possibly you realise that ducking a punch to the nose does not stop a kick elsewhere and so you enrol in a local martial arts club. Here you will learn that moving your arm in a certain way will deflect a punch and by means of much repetition, this block is imprinted on the cerebellum. Thereafter the action can be performed smoothly and accurately. The block should be practised against a punch so a strong association between the two is set up. This makes the response occur more quickly.

The more rapidly the visual stimulus is recognised and the response set in motion, the shorter is the 'Reaction time' which in this case is the time between the appearance of the moving fist and the block which deflects it.

The speed at which an impulse travels along a nerve fibre is fixed. No amount of training will make it go faster. However, repetition enhances the capacity of the synapse, so speed across it improves. Reducing the number of synapses to be crossed would also increase rate of transmission of the nerve impulse, and hence improve reaction time.

You will recall that the incoming signal was originally distributed to many parts of the brain. If the connections between these are sufficiently enhanced, then the signal may directly trigger a response from the motor cortex or ultimately, direct from the cerebellum itself.

By this means, reaction times may be reduced almost to those of escape reflexes, and these can be up to 6 times faster than responses which require recognition of the danger.

DISEASES OF THE NERVOUS SYSTEM

Throughout this chapter, I have referred to the effects of disease on certain functions. The number and variety of related diseases and the effects they produce are so vast that I can make only one comment. Each individual case must be dealt with on its own merits and the question asked, can any worthwhile martial arts training be undertaken? In my opinion, this should be judged very leniently as the improvement in quality of life for disabled people can be out of all proportion to the successes they achieve.

Epilepsy is a common disease. It is the result of a discharge of signals from a part of the cortex. These signals are so strong that they spread over the whole surface of the brain. The reason for this discharge is not known, though it can arise through irritation of a scar on the brain caused by a previous injury.

An epileptic fit consists of short, jerky movements which usually start in a limb and rapidly spread until they involve the whole of the body. The movements are powerful and quite unpredictable, lasting between 2 - 5 minutes. The sufferer becomes unconscious and this later passes into normal sleep. He then wakes up, apparently with no ill-effects and with no recollection of what has happened.

An epileptic fit can be a frightening thing to watch, and could upset the rest of the class. It is worth considering whether a condition for allowing an epileptic to train is that the rest of the class is informed about his disability.

The only harm which can come to an epileptic entering a fit is if he hurts himself when falling, or hits something during the fit. Epileptic martial artists should therefore train only on a good floor, and preferably on a padded one. The training surface must be completely free of dangerous projections such as radiators, wall bars, low windows, etc.

Chapter 8
THE GLANDS

Much of the internal workings of the body is controlled by what are called the 'Glands', and they act by means of chemical messengers which pass into the blood and are distributed throughout the body. The chemical messengers are known as Hormones. Of all the glands, only 4 have relevance to martial artists. These are:
- the *Pituitary* gland
- the *Adrenal* glands
- the *Pancreas*
- the sex glands (*Ovaries* and *Testes*)

THE PITUITARY GLAND
The pituitary is the gland which co-ordinates the activities of all the others. It is the only gland with an intimate nervous link to the brain. This means that the pituitary is in effect, under the control of the mid-brain, so the glandular system is able to respond to the outside environment.

THE ADRENALS
There are 2 adrenal glands, one above each kidney. They are stimulated both by the pituitary gland, and by the sympathetic nervous system. One of the hormones produced in the adrenals is *Adrenalin* and this has the same effect on the body as the sympathetic nerves; it prepares it to fight, or flight. Its effects are summarised thus:
- it increases heart rate
- it increase blood pressure
- it re-directs blood to the muscles
- it slows the digestion
- it increases fuel supply by breaking down glycogen to glucose.

The adrenal glands do not act as quickly as the sympathetic nervous system but their action last longer.

THE PANCREAS
The pancreas has already been mentioned in the chapter dealing with digestion. In addition to a digestive function, the pancreas also produces a hormone called *Insulin*. This regulates the usage of glucose in the body and its lack leads to high glucose levels in the blood. Excess glucose is removed by the kidneys and appears

in the urine. This is what happens in the disease known as *Diabetes*.

There are different kinds of diabetes but the only one which you are likely to find in the training hall is the 'Insulin dependent' type. As its name implies, regular does of insulin are needed to control it. Diabetes affects the whole of the sufferer's life, forcing him to strictly control both what he eats, and when he eats. The non-diabetic produces insulin in frequent, small amounts and this allows a very precise metering of blood glucose levels when environmental circumstances are changing. By way of comparison, the diabetic is obliged to take all his insulin in the form of one or two large doses each day.

An insulin coma sets in when blood glucose levels drop to a low level. It comes on in a matter of minutes whereas a diabetic coma (where blood sugar levels are too high) might take days to develop. The insulin coma is the only one you are likely to encounter in the training hall and though it can last several hours, it is rarely fatal. There are usually warning signs, such as a feeling of faintness, before the diabetic becomes unconscious.

Insulin coma can be quickly reversed by giving sugar or glucose. If glucose dissolved in water is given, the diabetic will regain consciousness in 1 - 2 minutes. Even if the glucose isn't swallowed, enough will be absorbed in the mouth to rouse him.

Nowadays, some diabetics carry an injection called Glucagon for usage in this situation. It might be wise if the coach learned how to administer it. Strenuous exercise uses a lot of glucose. Most diabetics know this and eat at the correct times, or take glucose tablets during training.

Some warning signs of insulin coma are varied and bizarre but they are always the same in any individual. Diabetics on insulin should have an insulin coma deliberately brought on, so they know what happens. This sort of information must be made known to the coach, so he can spot the onset of early symptoms and act before unconsciousness occurs. The coach must check with all diabetic students and confirm that there is something on hand to counter any big drop in blood glucose.

THE SEX GLANDS

The sex glands are the *Testes* in the male and the *Ovaries* in the female. Both are paired organs, producing hormones which, among other things, cause the appearance of what are called 'Secondary sexual characteristics'. These include such things as different distribution of body fat and hair, deeper voice in the male, and the development of breasts and menstruation in females.

The testes produce the hormone *Testosterone* and this is a naturally occurring form of *Anabolic steroid. Anabolic* is the term used to describe those substances which stimulate build-up of protein and therefore, of body tissues. This property has made anabolic steroids into one of the main artificial aides to training. In those sports where absolute strength is required, they may help by increasing bulk. This however, may be accompanied by a reduction in both speed and flexibility, so their usage in the martial arts is actually counter-productive.

There are 2 reasons why anabolic steroids should not be used. Firstly they run counter to the whole spirit of martial arts. Secondly, they have potentially serious side-effects, some of which:
□ cause temporary and sometimes permanent sterility
□ cause mascularisation of the female - growth of beard, deepening of voice etc.
□ cause an increase (sometimes permanent) in blood pressure
□ cause liver damage and occasionally cause development of liver cancers.

It is for all these reasons that the steroids are one of the groups for which martial artists are tested. So far, no user has been found, and I hope none ever will. Let me summarise the situation:
□ drugs conflict with the principles of martial art
□ drugs are potentially dangerous
□ drugs are of dubious benefit anyway

Being outside the body, the testes are rather vulnerable, and a kick landing on them is not an uncommon incident. Serious injury is rare, thanks to the testes' natural mobility. They work at a lower temperature than the rest of the body, and are supplied with muscles which reel them up and down, depending upon ambient temperature. Therefore a kick tends to displace, rather than squash them against underlying bone or muscle.

The testes can be ruptured. This is intensely painful, produces a great degree of shock and probably vomiting as well. The bag in which the testes rest - the *Scrotum* - becomes very bruised, and immediate admission to hospital is required.

It is difficult to protect the testes. The familiar plastic box restricts their movement and if pushed upwards, it squeezes them against the pelvic bones. Tight underpants also pose problems because they prevent the testes from moving with the impact. Unless a rigid box which does not move under impact can be devised, it is probably better that the testes are left to look after themselves.

As well as producing eggs, the ovaries produce the female sex hormones. Two of these, *Oestrogen* and *Progesterone*, are involved with the menstrual cycle. The first day of menstruation (the 'Period') is customarily defined as the first day of the cycle. On about day 4, the oestrogen level begins rising and this causes the lining of the womb to become thickened. On day 12 - 14, the ovary releases an egg and begins producing progesterone. This prepares the lining of the womb for a fertilised egg to be implanted. If this does not happen, then by day 28 the levels of both hormones drop sharply and the result of this is to shed the thick lining to the womb. This takes place with a certain amount of bleeding and an average blood loss of about 30 mls.

The stimulus for production of the ovarian hormones comes from the pituitary gland. As I mentioned before, the pituitary is closely connected to the mid-brain, so the emotions can and do have a significant effect upon the cycle. In some cases, menstruation can be completely suppressed. Conversely, the ovarian hormones affect the brain and the emotional state of women can alter noticeably in the days before menstruation starts. One thing is proven however, and that is during the week before a period is due to start, the female's reaction times become longer and she becomes much more accident-prone.

The only time a girl cannot become pregnant is when she is already pregnant. Very crudely, this is the basis for oral contraception ('the Pill'). The Pill contains hormones which fool the body into thinking it is pregnant. As a result of this, certain bodily changes which occur during pregnancy can also occur whilst taking the Pill.

These include the following:
- ☐ a reduction in basal metabolism, so that less food is needed
- ☐ the appetite is stimulated, so weight gain ensues
- ☐ reaction times slow
- ☐ the emotional state can change.

To be sure, these changes are not very noticeable in most individuals but the possibility that they may occur is worth bearing in mind.

The end of a woman's reproductive life (the *Menopause*) usually occurs between the ages of 45 - 55 years. As this end is reached, the amount of hormones produced do not rise high enough for their drop to cause menstruation. There are other effects, the important one for martial artists being a condition known as *Osteoporosis*. This causes a reduction in the amount of calcium within the bones, and a general reduction in the amount of bone in the body, making them more likely to fracture. This happens to a lesser degree in active women and in those cases where a good growth-spurt occurred at puberty.

While not a problem with practising martial artists,the menopause may be important in the case of new female students aged 40+. 'Hormonal Replacement Therapy' ('HRT') administers small doses of hormones to replace the loss of natural ones. This helps prevent osteoporosis.

Chapter 9
PSYCHOLOGY

So far I have dealt with the physical systems of the body, and how they react to training. Now it is time to consider that part of the body which is in charge – the mind. The mind is generally held to exist in the cortex of the brain, though quite where, no-one knows. Ambitions, expectations, imagination and all the thoughts which make up the mind are there.

To many people, the mind and body are completely separate things, but why should this be so? The mind may feel anger at something, so the body reacts with a flushed face, a rising pulse rate, and increased blood pressure and muscle tone. A friend of the opposite sex looks and feels especially good, so the senses of sight and touch send their messages to the brain and the result is a feeling of pleasure. Both of these situations show clearly that the mind and body are closely connected. In fact, they cannot be separated.

How does this affect the martial artist? In the following examples and situations, I have sometimes referred to top-class performers and international competitors. However, this has only been done because in these people, the effects are more noticeable.

IMAGINATION

Imagination is the seeing and feeling of events or situations which have not yet happened. This appears to be an in-built faculty which cannot be trained. Imagination in any individual is not something which can be appreciated by a third party such as the coach. There are some individuals on whom no amount of coaxing or encouragement appear to have the slightest effect. This may not be a lack of imagination; it could just be that person's inability to express his feelings and emotions.

Imagination is an important ingredient in the fostering of ambitions.

AMBITIONS & EXPECTATIONS

An ambition is the setting of a goal to be achieved in the future. Such goals may be reasonable, or unreasonable. It is unreasonable for a new student to set as his goal, the acquiring of a black belt within seven days of commencing training! It may be more reasonable for such a student to have the ambition to obtain a black belt in perhaps two years' time.

Ambition should be based upon experience. It might be that the 10 year old has seen a Bruce Lee film and wants to be like him, or perhaps the young woman who was nearly mugged wants to be able to defend herself. Whichever is the case, it is the job of the martial arts coach to discover the reasons for students joining the class, and the goals which they have set for themselves. The coach must be able to assess their separate ambitions in the light of their potential abilities and if necessary, get the students to re-evaluate their goals. Having adopted a mutually acceptable goal, the coach must next set down a series of intermediate targets, and construct training in such a way as to achieve them.

This may seem very complicated but it is fortunate that the majority of individuals in the martial arts class have similar ambitions and abilities, so a standard course can be devised. Nevertheless, there are those more brilliant or less talented than average, and the art of the coach is to identify this and modify the course to suit them.

We pass on now to discuss expectations. These are the feelings that, it is imagined, will follow the achievement of the desired goal. Whether these expectations are fulfilled or not has an effect upon the future of the martial artist. Each student has certain expectations upon joining a club and these will be as different as the number of students enrolled. One will be truly interested in the martial arts and want to learn them; another will just want to become fitter. A third student may just want the social environment provided by the club. If these various expectations are not realised, the student gives up and takes up another pastime.

This is not to say that the chap who has won the world championships finds it was not all it was cracked up to be, and therefore gives up martial art in favour of bowls! He may feel like doing just that for a time, but sooner or later his ambition is re-kindled by a different set of expectations.

The student who fails his black belt grading may excuse himself by saying "I had a cold," or "I was out drinking all last night." This provides a reason for failure and allows him to try again. On the other hand, the student who fails his very first grading is much more likely to drop out. It is therefore the job of the coach to ensure that no-one's expectations are set too high. In practical terms, it also means that a student should not be set a test which is beyond his capability.

CONFIDENCE

Confidence is the knowledge that a task can be performed, and that the right techniques will be chosen to accomplish it. Everyone has had the experience of seeing a student perform perfectly in training, yet on the day of the grading do nothing right. This is obviously not a lack of ability, it is a lack of confidence.

In the previous chapter, we noted that the learning of techniques is a function of the brain cortex. The cortex memorises certain stimuli and their consequences, and then forms an association between the two. A response is selected and a signal sent so that it is performed. The sequence of movements concerned in the response is also memorised in the cerebellum. In fact, a variety of stimuli and responses exist, so the brain cortex is obliged to choose between them.

The whole stimulus/response reaction has been classed as voluntary, semi-voluntary, or automatic. Confidence lies in abandoning voluntary control, whilst relying upon the automatic processing of stimulus and a direct output to the cerebellum. A task is performed slowly and perhaps not very well, when you are thinking about it. It was precisely this which caused the student to fail his grading. Lack of confidence made him rely on voluntary control of his actions.

The coach must be able to give the student confidence to perform to the best of his ability. The first requirement towards achieving this is the student's respect for the ability and truthfulness of the coach. The student must be taught to a certain level of skill and then made to understand that he has reached that level. The coach's skill lies in communicating this to the student and then by constantly reinforcing it by suggestion. The most usual way of achieving this is to repeat an opinion to the student until the latter comes to regard it as a fact. However, each coach must develop his own methods of confidence-building according to his own particular abilities and personality.

The coach must be aware that students each have their own

peculiarities of build and fitness, so the techniques taught must be flexible. The way in which they are taught must be adapted to suit the students' personalities.

A few words about communication are perhaps in order at this point. Communication is made by means of words and what is called 'Body language'. It is the latter that I will now refer to. Expressed simply, body language is the conveying of emotion, information and sometimes fact by facial expression, posture, and gestures. These all add up to a very potent method of communication. Body language is a deservedly much written-about subject, the scope of which is too wide for me to cover it in this book.

All coaches should learn about body language, though in fairness, many are already subconsciously aware of it. By understanding how it works, the coach can come to know the signals he is sending out and modify them to suit the occasion. Conflicts between what you say and what your body language reveals must be avoided. For example, it is no good telling someone that he is going to win a fight when your whole body seems to be suggesting that you expect him to be flattened in the first few seconds.

MOTIVATION
This is the desire to do well. In a recent competition, one team were better equipped than their opponents. They were physically fitter and technically better. The other team had a strong desire to perform well in front of a home crowd and this was sufficient to carry them to victory. The first team, through over-confidence, did not allow their reflexes full rein. The second team members all performed above themselves.

The latter statement is actually nonsense, of course, since no-one can do more than they are capable of. However, a martial artist performs to only 80 - 85% of his actual capabilities when he is turning in a 'normal best'. It is when he draws upon that remaining 15 - 20% that he is said to go above himself.

This concept goes beyond instilling confidence. It is putting into the students' minds the idea of greater benefit accruing to an extra-good performance. This benefit may take the form of the coach's greater satisfaction, or an increase in the students' self-esteem. The stimulus needed will vary from student to student.

Motivation must be done carefully. A highly motivated person also has high expectations and if he fails, or these expectations are not fulfilled, then the consequent distress will also be very great.

AGGRESSION

Aggression is the emotional state a person reaches when he wants to attack a particular target. This target need not be another human being! Aggression is common to everyone, though some individuals are more highly aggressive than others. Aggression has a physical side which derives from stimulation of the sympathetic nervous system (*see page 7.4*). A person in an aggressive state has a flushed face, the pulse rate and blood pressure are raised, and the muscles increase their tone in preparation for instant and rapid movement. In other words, the body is ready for combat.

In terms of martial arts practice, this may well be a good thing. It must however be borne in mind that martial art techniques are potentially very injurious, so aggression must be voluntarily curbed. Control of aggression by the brain is most important and the greater the aggression, the less control the brain has over it.

The level of aggression varies in any individual. Even the most timid of people can be roused to a fighting fury if suitably stimulated. In others, this state can be reached all too easily. A person who cannot control his aggression should not be allowed to train in the martial arts. The good coach will spot them at an early stage and weed them out.

RELAXATION

Relaxation of the mind is a very useful technique to acquire. It can remove worry, which is the enemy of confidence, and is very restful. If you can relax your mind for 10 minutes, it is worth a whole night's sleep. When the mind is relaxed, it is not blank. Thoughts follow no organised pattern and wander where they like. Think of the state as a sort of day-dream.

I believe that relaxation of this kind is a state of self-hypnosis. The subject of a hypnotic state is not asleep; he remains aware of his surroundings and his senses (especially hearing) are often abnormally acute. He is highly sensitive to suggestion and if this is repeated often enough, it will become fixed in the brain and acted upon. There is no question of the hypnotist imposing his will upon the subject. Any suggestion which goes against the subject's moral values or beliefs will be rejected and if it comes to a battle of wills, the subject will win by simply coming out of the trance.

Apart from this, the nature of the hypnotic state is not defined. I always think of it as the state between being awake and being asleep, when there is a dissociation between mind and body. Most people enter this state at some time or another, and experience a sensation of levitation, or of moving downwards.

The meditation practised in some of the martial arts is a form of self-hypnosis and the techniques which may be used are those which any hypnotist would recognise. These include:

☐ sounds :the repetition of a monotonous sound
   such as the 'Mantra'
☐ sights :fixing the eyes on one point,
   either near at hand or distant
☐ imagination :thinking of a sensation, such as lying in water
☐ movement :the repetition of monotonous movements,
   such as swaying backwards and forwards.

Relaxation, hypnosis and meditation amount to the same thing. The coach is well advised to learn something about them, preferably from a skilled practitioner. A word of warning; these techniques will not improve the students' skills!

ABNORMAL PSYCHOLOGY

Worry is not abnormal unless it is unnecessary and/or prolonged. Normal worry is useful because it concentrates the mind upon a problem which is hopefully then solved. When worry does anything else, then it becomes a *Neurosis*. It is my opinion that a healthy body is a great protector of the mind but where this protection fails, then relaxation techniques should be tried.

Tranquillisers and other drugs are fashionable, but they can lead to dependence and in any case, they cure nothing.

Depression produced by neither worry nor anxiety is only helped by skilled medical treatment. It is very unlikely that a genuinely depressed student would feel like training, and if he did, he would get no benefit from it.

Schizophrenia is the medical name for a 'Split mind'. This gives a clue to the nature of the illness. During an attack, the behaviour of a schizophrenic is so different from normal that it seems as though two minds were occupying the same skull. A characteristic of the disease is delusions. Delusions of a sensory nature are known as 'Hallucinations'. The sufferer may hear voices telling him to do something. Joan of Arc was probably a schizophrenic and the man who believes himself to be Napoleon certainly is a schizophrenic. Some suffer from delusions of persecution and this can lead them into violent and dangerous behaviour. It is for this reason that schizophrenics should never be trained in the martial arts. The difficulty is that many schizophrenics pass unseen.

A *Psychopath* is a person without sense of social responsibility. He does exactly what he wants, when he wants and has no regard for the consequences of his actions. He may inflict pain but derives no pleasure from it. In fact he is completely indifferent. The psychopath can often be detected by noting his completely anti-social behaviour. He can be very dangerous and under no circumstances should he be taught the martial arts. If a coach has any suspicion that a student is a schizophrenic or a psychopath, he should seek expert advice immediately.

I strongly recommend that all martial arts coaches use a period of provisional membership, when the overall performance of students can be monitored. During this time, no techniques of a practical nature should be taught.

Chapter 10
TRAINING CHILDREN

The training of children is a specialised subject. Children are not miniature adults and must not be treated as such. The two obvious differences between children and adults are firstly that children are much smaller, and secondly that they are sexually immature.

NUTRITION

Many martial art coaches organise residential courses lasting between 5 and 15 days. The trend is nowadays for many children to participate in them. The coach must not forget that he is responsible for their welfare whilst they are away from the loving bosom of their family and with this very much in mind, I am penning this section on the care and feeding of budding young martial artists. Now read on!

Children need to take in a large amount of food because they are growing, and at certain times, they grow very rapidly indeed. Their surface area is proportionally much greater than adults. This means that they lose more heat through their skin. Nutritionally speaking, the child therefore needs to take in sufficient high-energy foods such as fats and carbohydrates, and enough building materials in the form of proteins, to cope with demands. Having said that, the overall balanced diet is probably very much the same as for the adult:

□ 30% protein
□ 30% fat
□ 40% carbohydrate

Total calorie intake will be high in proportion to size and even a small child will eat as much as an adult. 2,500 Cals is not an excessive requirement and during growth in the upper age range, demand may equal that needed by a martial artist in training, i.e., around 4,000 Cals.

Children also need a reasonable amount of fibre and minerals. The increasing volume of blood needs extra iron and new bones must have calcium to make them hard. Vitamins are also very important. Fat soluble vitamins A and D are in demand for the production of good skin, connective tissue and bone. Water soluble vitamins B and C are needed to cope with the growth of nerves, and the child's high metabolic rate.

A recent research project showed that a group of average

children who were given vitamin supplements performed better in intelligence tests. This does not however, prove that children need supplements; only that they were on a poor diet to start with.

Two other facts are worth mentioning: an active 6 - 8 year old may be too involved to stop and eat a meal. If he is stopped and made to eat, it is more than likely he will fiddle about until he can resume his activities. Hunger sets in before his next meal is due and if a 'no eating between meals' rule is applied, he will be starved.

A group of children were shut up in a room with plenty to entertain them and lots of different foodstuffs. The latter included nutritionally good food as well as junk food. The children were told to take as much as they liked, of what they liked. A record was then taken of what each child chose and when this was analysed, it was discovered that each had selected an adequate and well-balanced diet, containing sufficient minerals and vitamins. The moral seems to be that given the choice, a child will pick for himself a good and adequate diet.

RESPIRATION & CIRCULATION
It is difficult to improve on the respiratory and circulatory systems that a child already possesses. It is easier for you to appreciate this when little Jackie is training like mad and chattering all the time, while you plod on and wonder where the next breath is coming from. However, martial arts training can teach children how to breathe correctly, and this can be a great benefit in later life.

MUSCLES
A child's muscles are growing and getting stronger all the time. Some strengthening exercises may do no harm but you must be aware that young, growing tissues are more fragile than adult ones, and so can be damaged more easily. Children have a good aerobic capacity and this is not adversely affected by the correct type of training. However, childrens' muscles have very little anaerobic capacity and this cannot be trained in by exercise. This means that a child can only sustain hard training for a short while, and explosive effort can be kept up for a few seconds only, if at all. This is not because the child is lazy, the task is simply beyond his capacity.

Anaerobic capacity is developed from puberty on, so until that stage is reached, training must be of an aerobic type only.

THE SKELETON

Some of the most dramatic differences between the child and the adult are seen in the skeleton. When the bones are first laid down, they are made only of tough but flexible cartilage. This is gradually replaced by bone. Bone growth begins at the middle in what is called a 'Centre of Ossification' and from there, it grows towards both ends. At the time of birth, many, but not all of the bones have started the process of changing into bone (*Fig. 36*). The tibia is about 75 millimetres long at birth and must grow to a final length of between 300 - 375 millimetres. If the whole length of bone ossified in one go, growth would be very difficult to achieve.

Other centres develop at the ends of the bone and these form the joints with neighbouring bones. Therefore a child's bones

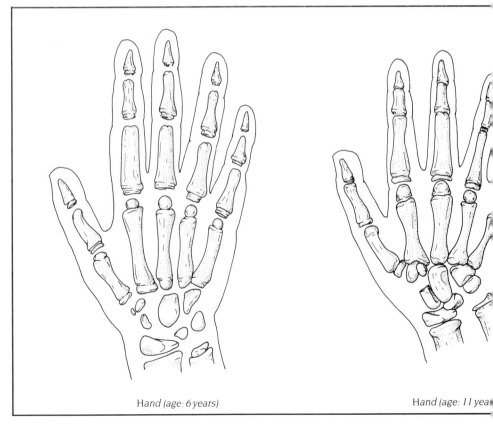

Hand (age: 6 years)   Hand (age: 11 years)

consist of a bony shaft, with cartilage at either end, capped with bony end-plates. All growth is taking place at the junction of the shaft with the cartilage. As bone grows into the cartilage, more cartilage is laid down. This process continues until the bones reach their final size at the age of 16 years in girls, and 18 in boys.

If the growing points of the bone are damaged, then that bone will grow no further. Blood supply to the growing points comes via the bone shaft and if this is disturbed, then rate of growth slows. If so much shearing force is applied that the cartilage/bone shaft junction is actually displaced, then blood supply is interrupted and the bone ossifies completely at its existing length. Luckily this is uncommon because cartilage is elastic and bends quite easily.

It can nevertheless happen at the lower end of the radius, with the result that the wrist joint becomes angled and in extreme cases, the hand can point inwards, almost at a right angle to the

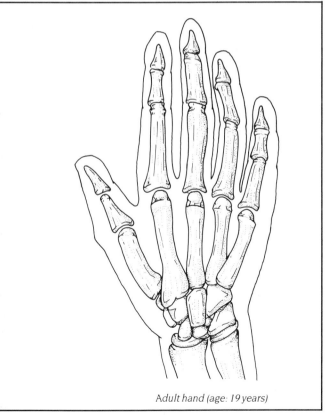

**Fig. 36
A comparison of bone formation in wrist and hand bones**

Adult hand (age: 19 years)

arm. As well as being unsightly, this is not very useful.

There are three other conditions where blood supply to growing bones can be interrupted. In each case, the normal processes of repair operate:

□ dead and damaged tissues are absorbed

□ fibrous tissue replaces them

□ new bone grows into the site.

The symptoms in each case are similar - tenderness and swelling over the affected bone and pain particularly on movement. The time these conditions take to heal depends entirely upon how well they are rested. Any disturbance of the tissues as they repair will cause further tissue-death and put the healing process almost back to the beginning.

The least common of these conditions is that which affects the foot. The bone affected is on the inner side of the foot, at the top of the arch. Immobilisation in a plaster cast may be needed. This is likely to be followed by arthritis of the surrounding joints.

The commonest form affects the tibia. There is an extra centre of ossification on the front of the tibia, at the point where the quadriceps tendon is attached and contraction of that muscle tends to pull this upwards. Excessive pulling bends the cartilage and may interrupt blood supply. This condition rejoices in the name of Osgood - Schlatter's Disease. It is most common in 13 - 15 year old boys who play rugby or soccer and there is as yet no information on whether it is also caused by martial art training.

Osgood - Schlatter's disease may take up to 18 months to heal. This is not because it is a serious condition - quite the reverse in fact. It is actually the least serious of the three, since it has no after-effects. The reason lies in the fact that it is well nigh impossible to persuade an active 14 year old that he should not ride his bike or play football for at least three months. Sometimes the only way is to encase the leg in a plaster cast.

Perthe's disease is the most serious. It affects the hip and causes the death of the head of the femur. As this is a weight-bearing joint, the softened bone quickly deforms. This damages the pelvic part of the joint to the extent that the whole joint becomes nearly flat. Any weight then causes the joint to dislocate. Prompt diagnosis is the only way that this can be avoided. First sign is a limp. This appears days before any pain begins. It is of vital importance that any unexplained limp is treated seriously and no weight-bearing is allowed until the joint has been examined under X-rays. Perthe's disease is treated by bed rest and traction, for even the tone of the resting muscles is sufficient to deform the head of the femur.

Eventually the head is completely reformed. However, early onset of arthritis is an invariable consequence of Perthe's disease.

Just to confuse matters, there is another condition called 'Irritable hip'. This starts in the same way as Perthe's disease but the few days of bed rest whilst waiting for X -ray examination are enough to cure it. The cause is unknown.

The reason I have discussed these is that there is life outside of the training hall. Any active 10 - 16 year old will be involved in many and various physical activities. I did a small survey of children training in a martial art during the course of which, I gave 50 children a superficial examination of their musculo-skeletal system. I found 37 different abnormalities (some children had more than one), the majority of which were trivial. Four were potentially serious. There is no evidence to suggest that these injuries were caused by martial art training but the disturbing fact was that the coach was unaware of two-thirds of them, including three of the four serious ones.

In my opinion, it should be a duty of the coach to enquire whether anyone has an injury, or any other aches and pains. He may not be told, but at least he tried.

A child's joints are naturally flexible. A child of 8 should be able to turn his head through 120 degrees on each side, whereas an adult might manage 90 degrees. This is because children's ligaments are very elastic, and their bones consist in part of cartilage, allowing a little movement. However, these young tissues are fragile and may be easily damaged if they are taken to or beyond their limits. Some children are stiff, as I found in my little survey but this results from muscle tension. It is far better to accept a slightly lower level of flexibility than risk damage to growing ligaments and joints by over-stretching them.

Some martial arts classes expect children to perform press-ups on their knuckles or fingertips. Both of these practices should cease. Joint locks should never be applied to children and breaking techniques must not be practised.

GLANDS

As I said at the beginning of this chapter, the two obvious differences between children and adults are size and sexual immaturity. Growth does not continue at a steady rate throughout childhood. Each child will have two or three periods when they grow faster. These are called 'Growth spurts'. Girls have them between 5 - 8 and boys a little later at 8 - 10 years. This is why girls are often larger and stronger than boys of the same age. This is important when matching partners for training and sparring etc. Coaches should match them by size, not by age (*Fig. 37*).

Training affects growth. This is most easily seen in Eastern European girl gymnasts. These children were taken at the age of 8 - 10 and trained hard in skill and general fitness. As a result of this, Pituitary gland activity is is suppressed and there is a reduction in growth. Energy intake has been diverted from growth into physical activity. This loss of growth is never made up and many of these

Fig. 37 A comparison of growth between boys and girls of similar ages

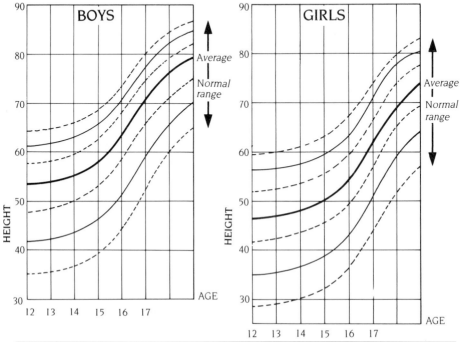

gymnasts did not reach 150 centimetres in height when adult. This is an extreme example but it does show the effect that excessive training in any activity can have.

The development of sexual maturity at puberty marks the last of the major growing periods. During it, the girl will gain 15 kilos and the boy, 25 kilos. This is about half of their total weight gain from the age of 6. This again has a relevance to matching training partners. A girl of 14 will probably be bigger, better co-ordinated, have more stamina and perhaps more strength than a boy of the same age. This state of affairs does not become reversed until about the age of 16.

A rather less obvious result of this growth spurt is that the child's visualisation of his own body can become defective. He might find his hand or foot a couple of inches further away than he thought. This makes the child seem clumsy, and explains a sudden deterioration in performance during training.

Over-training affects the onset of puberty, and can delay it by as much as 2 - 3 years. Whilst this occurs in both sexes, it is most obvious in girls. Their hips do not broaden and breasts are not developed. In some cases, menstruation is delayed until the age of 18. The pubertal growth spurt is delayed by an equivalent period but by the time it begins, the bones have completely ossified and no further growth is possible.

I think it is unlikely that children would be trained to this degree in the martial arts, but certainly some children become obsessive about training, so a knowledge of the effects of over-training is essential.

PSYCHOLOGY

Of the 50 children in my little survey (*see above*), two were 5 years of age, three were 15 and the majority were between 9 and 12 years old. It may then be possible to say that those who start before the age of 12, do not carry on. This may be because training does not satisfy them and they find it boring.

A child basically learns through play. It is therefore advisable that any form of teaching, no matter how serious the purpose, should be made into a game. On average, a child will concentrate on one thing for about 4 minutes before becoming bored and wanting some new activity. A training session for children should therefore be a series of games. There would be a warm-up game, stretching games, a self-defence game and a little formal practice mixed in the form of short spells to maintain interest.

Teach a child something new and he will learn it quickly. Unlike an adult, however, he will not then practise the new skill to get it right. He always wants to learn something new. Another character-istic of children is that they cannot cope with failure. When he fails to achieve a goal, he doesn't keep trying until he succeeds. Instead he goes off and finds something which he can succeed in.

This applies to grading examinations. If a child fails, he will take up table tennis instead. Grading standards for children should therefore be very flexible. It may be necessary to insert a great number of steps up the ladder, from one belt to the next, but there should never be any steps down.

To summarise:
□ a child learns new techniques very quickly
□ a child is very interested in anything new
□ a child lacks concentration.

Be aware of and act on these facts and you will retain the younger members of the class.

A child has no ambitions or aspirations of his own. He will take these instead from parents, or from respected teachers. If he thinks that he has failed to live up to their expectations, guilt at letting someone down is added to a sense of failure and the child will find that burden intolerable. It is for that reason I consider competition for children under the age of 16 years to be wrong. It may be good for the egos of the coach or parents, but it could equally well be disastrous for the child.

INDEX